ARYAN SUN-MYTHS

ARYAN SUN-MYTHS

THE ORIGIN OF RELIGIONS

WITH AN INTRODUCTION BY

CHARLES MORRIS

AUTHOR OF "A MANUAL OF CLASSICAL LITERATURE," AND "THE ARYAN RACE: ITS ORIGIN AND ITS ACHIEVEMENTS."

LONDON
TRÜBNER & CO., LUDGATE HILL
1889
All Rights Reserved

PRINTED IN THE U.S.A.

PREFACE.

THE attention of the writer having been called to the fact that all Indo-Germanic nations have worshipped crucified Saviours, an investigation of the subject was made. Overwhelming proof was obtained that the sun-myths of the ancient Aryans were the origin of the religions in all of the countries which were peopled by the Aryans. The Saviours worshipped in these lands are personifications of the Sun, the chief god of the Aryans. That Pagan nations worshipped a crucified man, was admitted by the Fathers of the early Christian Church. The holy Father Minucius Felix, in his *Octavius*, written as late as A. D. 211, indignantly resents the supposition that the sign of the cross should be considered as exclusively a Christian symbol; and represents his advocate of the Christian argument as retorting on an infidel opponent thus: "As for the adoration of crosses, which you object to against us, I must tell you that we neither adore crosses nor desire them. You it is, ye Pagans, who worship wooden gods, who are the most likely people to adore wooden crosses, as being parts of the same substance with your deities. For what else are your ensigns, flags, and standards, but crosses gilt and beautified? Your victorious trophies not only represent a simple cross, but a cross with a man upon it." Tertullian, a Christian Father of the second and third centuries, writing to the Pagans, says: "The origin of your gods is derived from figures moulded on a cross. All those rows of images on your standards are the appendages of crosses; those hangings on your standards and banners are the robes of crosses" (*Egyptian Belief*, p. 217). Arrian, in his *History of Alexander*, states that the troops of Porus, in their war with Alexander the Great, carried on their standards the figure of a man. Justin Martyr, in his Dialogue with Trypho, says that there exist not a people, civilized or semi-civilized, who have not offered up prayers in the name of a crucified Saviour to the Father and Creator of all things. Eusebius, the ecclesiastical historian, says that the names of Jesus and Christ were both known and honored among the ancients (*Eccl. Hist.*, lib. i. chap. iv.). We find Saint Paul avowing that he was made a minister of the gospel, which had been preached to every creature under heaven (Col. i. 23). For centuries after the time assigned as the birth of Jesus, he was not represented as a man on a cross. The earliest representation of him was as a lamb (*History of our Lord in Art*, Vol. I.). This custom continued until the pontificate of Agathon (A. D. 608), during the reign of Constantine Pogonatus. By the Sixth Synod of Constantinople (Canon 82), it was ordained that instead of the ancient symbol which had been the lamb, the figure of a man nailed to a cross should be represented. All this was confirmed by Pope Adrian I. (Dupuis's *Origin of Religious Belief*, p. 252; also Higgins's *Anacalypsis*, Vol. II. p. 3).

The writer makes no claim to originality, excepting in the arrangement of this work. The endeavor has been simply to condense what has been obtained from other works.

The original intention was to give a brief sketch, with an appended list of works from which the material was taken; but on making an addition to the book it was deemed best to give references. The references for the original sketch will be found at the end of the book.

The writer has been favored in having an Introduction by one so familiar with the subject as Mr. Charles Morris, author of *The Aryan Race*.

BOSTON, February, 1889.

TABLE OF CONTENTS.

	PAGE
INTRODUCTION	11
LIST OF BOOKS CONSULTED	21
ARYAN SUN-MYTHS THE ORIGIN OF RELIGIONS	27
Appendix A	147
Appendix B	153
Appendix C	158
Appendix D	159
Appendix E	166
Appendix F	170
Reference Notes	179
Index	189

INTRODUCTION.

It seems, at first glance, remarkable with what readiness the Teutonic and Celtic tribes dropped their ancestral faiths and accepted Christianity, now through the persuasions of a missionary, now at the bidding of a chief. But a fuller study of the subject renders the unusual ease of this conversion much less surprising, by making it apparent that they rather added the leading dogmas of Christianity to their old faiths than replaced the latter by the former. They ceased to worship Odin and the lesser deities, and began to worship Christ, the Virgin, and the saints; but they invested the latter with many of the attributes of the former, retained most of their old religious dogmas and ceremonies, and converted primitive Christianity quite as much as they were converted by it. The conversion was, indeed, as much a change of names as of beliefs. Though the ethics of Christianity slowly leavened this swarming mass of barbarism, the theology of the new faith became so closely interwoven with that of the old that it is not easy to this day to separate them.

The nineteenth-century critical study of religious beliefs and the progress of the science of comparative mythology have gone far towards clearing up this mystery of the past, and are leading the way to a science of comparative theology, as students break through the artificial barrier of sacredness which has been raised around this or that system of belief, and dare to question where older students deemed it their duty to adore. It is being more and more widely held that no belief can be sacred, that all faith must rest either upon evidence or blind acceptance, and that they who base their belief upon a study of facts are far superior intellectually, and certainly equal morally, to those who accept dogmas upon authority. Faith has been covered with a veil which it was declared impious to lift, and the very word exalted into a kind of magic formula, which was deemed powerful enough to move mountains. But what is faith, critically considered? It is either an unquestioning acceptance of the assertions of ancient books and modern teachers, which the reasoning powers of the individual are autocratically forbidden to deal with; or it is a belief reached through doubt and question, the persistent study of facts and the fullest exercise of the intellect. In the latter case it is the actual belief of the individual; in the former, the belief of somebody else, which has been instilled into the receptive mind of the disciple, and before whose sacredness every intrusive doubt and irreconcilable fact must bow the head in worship.

This dogma is a relic of the Dark Ages. It is based upon the general ignorance which prevailed in ancient communities and their restful dependence upon the superior learning of their teachers. It is utterly out of accordance with the general education of modern peoples, and the spirit of research which is now everywhere active, and which is far too vigorous to be repelled by the highest fence of theological interdict.

The study of the mythological systems of ancient nations has revealed many curious and unlooked-for facts and correspondences. It has been made apparent, in the first place, that those mythologies had their origin in primitive ideas about the movements of the heavenly bodies, the variations of day and night, summer and winter, and other natural phenomena, which were in time, through the modification of human ideas, transformed into the doings of a throng of deific beings. The worshippers did not know whence came their gods. We, who can approach the subject without prejudice and bigotry, and to whom mythology has ceased to be sacred, can easily trace their origin, and point out nearly every step of their unfoldment. It has become evident, in the second place, that a close affinity exists between the mythological ideas of different and often widely separated countries, the resemblance extending not only to their broader features, but in some cases to their minor details of dogma and belief. This correspondence in belief is undoubtedly due to two causes; primarily to the fact that the steps of unfoldment of the human intellect and the growth of ideas have been closely similar in all civilizing peoples; and secondly to the intercourse of tribes and nations, and the outflow of ideas over the earth, by the several methods of peaceful interchange of views, warlike conquest and forcible conversion, and propagandism by missionary efforts. These various influences have tended to bring into some degree of conformity the religious systems not only of Europe, Asia, and Africa, but also those of the Old and the New World, between which some communication very probably existed in ancient times.

The primary religious ideas of all peoples were undoubtedly much the same. The unquestioned supremacy of the sun among the heavenly bodies, the striking changes to which it was subjected in the variation from day to night, and from summer to winter; its life-giving beneficence, and its seeming struggle with the demons of storm and cold; not only everywhere exalted this heavenly body into the position of king of the gods in every system of nature-worship, but gave rise to numerous myths, which necessarily in some measure corresponded, since they were everywhere based on the same phenomena of nature. It is true that nature-worship was not the sole primitive religious conception of mankind. Various other general ideas made their way into and influenced systems of belief, prominent among these being the custom of ancestor worship, which widely, perhaps universally, prevailed in developing nations, and exerted a vigorous influence upon unfolding religions. Mythology, however, occupies the most prominent position in the growth of religious beliefs. Ancestral and other systems of worship have influenced religious practice and ceremony to a marked extent, but have had much less to do with the growth of dogma than the intricate details of the history of the gods, to which the numerous phenomena of nature gave rise. Over religious belief the sun has exercised a dominant influence, and still faintly yet distinguishably shines through the most opaquely obscure of modern theological dogmas.

The work to which I am gratified in being requested to append these introductory remarks, is designed to point out in detail the correspondences of religious dogma to which I have alluded. How well or ill it does so may be left for readers to decide; but as a reader having some previous acquaintance with the subject, I should say that it has done so remarkably well, and that it would not be easy to make a stronger, fuller, and clearer presentation of the facts in so limited a space. The subject is one worthy of a much more extended treatment.

The only bone of contention in the work is its inclusion of the dogmas of Christianity among mythological outgrowths. And yet very few of these dogmas are the direct fruit of Christ's teachings. Very many of them are the work of later theologians, who were influenced both by their own religious education and the demands of their congregations. Christianity arose among the Jews, a people whose religious system had never been strongly mythological, and had become much less so in the course of time. But the new doctrine was not accepted by the Jews. It found its chief converts among peoples of Aryan origin,—the Greeks, the Romans, the Teutons, the Celts, etc.,—peoples among whom mythology had become extraordinarily developed, and whom it was simply impossible to convert in a mass to radically new ideas. They accepted Christ and his moral teachings, with the skilfully organized church system of the primitive Christians; but their older mythological belief was not worn as a cloak to be thrown off at will, but was rather a plant whose roots had penetrated to every fibre of their beings, and had become an intimate part of the texture of their minds. It strongly influenced the most learned among them. With the unlearned it continued the prevalent system of belief, and insinuated itself into the dogmas of the new church with a power impossible to resist. It may be repeated that the Christian theology of to-day was not born with Christ and his apostles. Its growth was slow. Traditions arose, partly based on old myths, partly on misconceptions of Christ's life and teachings, which affected even the writers of the several lives of Christ, and more strongly those who were farther removed from Christ.

From the very start legendary dogmas of mythological origin seem to have arisen in the new church, to have become the firm beliefs of congregations, and to have affected the minds of theologians much more than they themselves were aware of. And as the new faith spread through the world, it became more and more imbued with old thought, until mythology became the woof of that system of which morality was the warp.

Christianity, properly considered, is not a system of belief, but a system of ethics. Christ taught no creed. His life was spent in the inculcation of lofty ideas of morality. The few dogmas which he did assert are full of evidence of the influence of the preceding Hebrew faith, and were doubtless the outcome of his early religious education. Many of his utterances have been tortured into creeds, but few of them bear the interpretations that have been laid upon them. He was a moral teacher, pure and simple, and as an inculcator of moral ideas he stands at the summit of mankind. His teachings are the simplest and loftiest, his life was the noblest and most self-sacrificing, that literature and history present to our gaze. But for the dogmas of Christianity he is not responsible. They grew up after his death, through the slow years and centuries, under the influence of a host of more ancient ideas and mythological conceptions, and the bulk of them have no more to do with the Christianity taught by Christ than has the mythology of the Aztecs. Christianity was simply thrown into a world seething with religious beliefs and fancies, and could not but take up some accretion of these prevailing ideas, which gathered around it like clouds around the sun. The pure light of Christ's teachings lay within, but was long almost lost in the obscuring doctrine that belief is the essential of virtue, conduct a minor accessory; that lapse from virtue may be readily pardoned, lapse from faith is unpardonable. Such a doctrine has done infinite mischief to the cause of Christianity. Fortunately it is ceasing to prevail. The sun is burning through the clouds, and the example of Christ's life and the loftiness of his precepts are becoming of more value in religion than the creeds advanced by later theologians; and we may look forward with hope to the time in which conduct will become the essential feature of religion, and faith be relegated to its true position in the history of human thought.

CHARLES MORRIS.

BOOKS

From which the author has obtained information.

Anacalypsis	G. Higgins, F.R.A.S.
An Analysis of Egyptian Mythology	J. C. Pritchard, M.D.
An Analysis of the Historical Records of Ancient Egypt	J. C. Pritchard, M.D.
An Analysis of Religious Belief	Viscount Amberly.
Ancient Ecclesiastical History of Socrates Scholasticus	Trans. by J. Hammer, D.D.
Ancient Egypt under the Pharaohs	John Kenrick, M.A.
Ancient Faiths and Modern	Thomas Inman, M.D.
Ancient Faiths embodied in Ancient Names	Thomas Inman, M.D.
Ancient Pagan and Modern Christian Symbolism	Thomas Inman, M.D.
Ancient Symbol Worship	H. M. Westropp.
Antiquities of Mexico	Lord Kingsborough.
Antiquities of the Jews	Flavius Josephus.
Asiatic Researches	Asiatic Society.
Assyrian Discoveries	George Smith.
Bell's New Pantheon	J. Bell.
Bible Myths	T. William Doane.
Biographies of Words and the Home of the Aryas	Max Müller.
Buddha and Early Buddhism	Arthur Lillie.
Buddhism	J. H. Titcomb, D.D.

Chips from a German Workshop . .	*Max Müller.*
Christianity in China, Tartary, and Thibet	*E. R. Huc.*
Cory's Ancient Fragments of the Phœnician, Carthaginian, Babylonian, Egyptian, and other Authors . . .	*Cory.*
Curious Myths of the Middle Ages .	*Rev. S. Baring-Gould.*
Darwinism in Morals	*Frances P. Cobbe.*
Eastern Monachism	*R. Spence Hardy.*
Egyptian Belief and Modern Thought .	*James Bonwick.*
Egyptian Mythology and Egyptian Christianity	*Samuel Sharpe.*
Encyclopædia Britannica	*Ninth edition.*
Evidence as to Man's Place in Nature .	*Thomas H. Huxley, F.R.S., F.L.S.*
Fairy Tales: Their Origin and Meaning	*J. T. Bunce.*
Fusang	*Charles G. Leland.*
God in History	*C. K. von Bunsen.*
Hebrew and Christian Records . . .	*J. A. Giles.*
Hinduism	*Monier Williams, M.A.*
History of Ancient Sanscrit Literature	*Max Müller.*
History of China	*Thomas Thornton.*
History of Cornelius Tacitus	*C. Tacitus.*
History of Herodotus	*Herodotus.*
History of Hindostan	*Thomas Maurice.*
History of our Lord in Art	*Mrs. Jameson and Lady Eastlake.*
History of the Conflict between Religion and Science	*J. W. Draper, D.D.*
History of the Conquest of Mexico . .	*W. H. Prescott.*
History of the Decline and Fall of the Roman Empire	*Edward Gibbon.*
History of the Doctrine of the Deity of Jesus Christ	*Albert Réville.*

India, Ancient and Modern	*Rev. D. O. Allen.*
India, What can it Teach us?	*Max Müller.*
Indian Antiquities	*Thomas Maurice.*
Indian Wisdom	*Monier Williams, M.A.*
Koran	*Trans. by G. Sale.*
Lectures on the History of the Jewish Church	*Dean Stanley.*
Lectures on the Origin and Growth of Religion	*Max Müller.*
Lectures on the Origin and Growth of Religion	*P. Le Page Renouf.*
Lectures on the Pentateuch and Moabite Stone	*J. W. Colenso, D.D.*
Lectures on the Science of Language	*Max Müller.*
Life and Religion of the Hindoos	*J. C. Gangooly.*
Man's Earliest History	*Richard Owen.*
Manual of Buddhism	*R. S. Hardy.*
Manual of Mythology	*Alex. S. Murray.*
Monumental Christianity	*J. P. Lundy.*
Mysteries of Adoni	*S. F. Dunlap.*
Mythology among the Hebrews	*Ignaz Goldziher.*
Mythology of Ancient Greece and Italy	*T. Keightley.*
Mythology of the Aryan Nation	*Sir George W. Cox.*
Myths and Myth-Makers	*John Fiske.*
Myths and Rites of the British Druids	*Edwin J. Davis.*
Myths of the Middle Ages	*Rev. S. Baring-Gould.*
Myths of the New World	*Daniel Brinton.*
New Researches in Ancient History	*C. F. Volney.*
Northern Antiquities	*P. H. Mallet.*
Oriental Religions	*Samuel Johnson.*
Persia	*Frederick Shoberl.*
Prehistoric Times	*Sir John Lubbock.*
Primitive Culture	*Edward Burnett Tylor.*
Prolegomena of the History of Religion	*Albert Réville.*

Religions of India	*Auguste Barth.*
Researches into the Early History of Mankind	*E. B. Tylor.*
Rgya Cher-rol-pa, Thibetan version of the Sanskrit Lalita-vistara	*Foucaux (Ed.).*
Rig-Veda-Sanhita	*Max Müller.*
Roman Antiquities	*C. K. Dillaway.*
Sŏd, the Son of the Man	*S. F. Dunlap.*
Tales of Ancient Greece	*Sir George W. Cox.*
Taylor's Fragments	*Charles Taylor.*
The Ancient City	*F. G. Colanges.*
The Angel-Messiah of Buddhists, Essenes, and Christians	*Ernest de Bunsen.*
The Aryan Race	*Charles Morris.*
The Celtic Druids	*G. Higgins, F.R.A.S.*
The Chaldean Account of Genesis	*George Smith.*
The Chinese	*J. F. Davis.*
The Christ of Paul	*George Reber.*
The Descent of Man	*Charles Darwin.*
The Devil: his Origin, Greatness, and Decadence	*Albert Réville.*
The Diogesis	*Robert Taylor.*
The Epistle of Polycarp to the Philippians	*Trans. by Wake.*
The Essenes	*C. D. Ginsburg, LL.D.*
The First Book of Hermas	*Hermas.*
The Gnostics and their Remains	*C. W. King, M.A.*
The Gospel of the Infancy of Jesus Christ	*Apocryphal.*
The Great Cities of the Ancient World	*T. A. Buckley.*
The Heathen Religion	*J. P. Gross.*
The Legend of Samson	*H. Steinthal.*
The Legends and Theories of the Buddhists	*R. S. Hardy.*
The Life of Christ	*F. W. Farrar.*

The Life of Constantine	*Eusebius.*
The Life of Jesus Critically Examined	*David Strauss.*
The Light of Asia	*Edwin Arnold.*
The Lily of Israel	*L'Abbé Gerbet.*
The Martyrdom of Jesus of Nazareth	*Dr. I. M Wise.*
The Origin and Development of Religious Belief	*Rev. S. Baring-Gould.*
The Origin of All Religious Worship	*Charles F. Dupuis.*
The Poems of Æschylus	*Tr. by R. Potter, M.A.*
The Principles of Sociology	*Herbert Spencer.*
The Protevangelion	*Protevangelion Apoc.*
The Races of Man	*Oscar Peschel.*
The Religion of the Ancient Greeks	*Septchenes.*
The Religions of the World	*F. D. Maurice.*
The Rosicrucians	*H. Jennings.*
The Sacred Anthology	*M. D. Conway.*
The Science of Religion	*Max Müller.*
The Secret of the East	*Felix L. Oswald.*
The Serpent Symbol	*E. G. Squire.*
The Stratification of Language	*Max Müller.*
The Symbolical Language of Ancient Art and Mythology	*R. P. Knight.*
The Vishnu Purana	*Trans. by H. H. Wilson.*
Travels in Georgia, Persia, etc.	*Sir R. K. Porter.*
Tree and Serpent Worship	*James Fergusson, F.R.S.*
Types of Mankind	*S. G. Morton.*
Upanishads	*Trans. by Max Müller.*
Vestiges of the Spirit-History of Man	*S. F. Dunlap.*

ARYAN SUN-MYTHS

THE ORIGIN OF RELIGIONS.

The results obtained from the examination of language in its several forms leaves no room for doubt, Max Müller tells us, that there was a stage, in the history of human speech, during which the abstract words in constant use among ourselves were utterly unknown, when men had formed no notions of virtue or prudence, of thought and intellect, of slavery or freedom, but spoke only of the man who was strong, who could point the way to others and choose one thing out of many, of the man who was not bound to any other, and able to do as he pleased.

Language without words denoting abstract qualities implies a condition of thought in which men were only awakening to a sense of the objects which surrounded them, and points to a time when the world was to them full of strange sights and sounds, — some beautiful, some bewildering, some terrific; when, in short, people knew little of themselves beyond the vague consciousness of existence, and nothing of the phenomena of the world without.

In such a state they could but attribute to all

that they saw or touched or heard, a life which was like their own in its consciousness, its joys, and its sufferings. The varying phases of that life were therefore described as truthfully as human feelings or sufferings, and hence every phase became a picture, which remained intelligible as long as the conditions remained unchanged. In time, however, the conditions were changed. Men advanced in knowledge and civilization, and no longer thought of nature as possessing life and consciousness like their own.

In ancient times there lived, it is supposed on the highest elevation of Central Asia, a noble race of men, called the Aryan. Speaking a language not yet Sanskrit, Greek, or German, but containing the dialects of all, this clan which had advanced to a state of agricultural civilization had recognized the bonds of blood, and sanctioned the bonds of marriage. That they worshipped Nature, — the sun, moon, sky, earth, — a comparison of ancient religions and mythology in the lands peopled by Aryans, demonstrates. Their chief object of adoration was the Sun. To this race, in the infancy of its civilization, the Sun was not a mere luminary, but a Creator, Ruler, Preserver, and Saviour of the world.

As there could be no life or vegetation without light, the Sun, as a light-bringer, becomes Creator, and if Creator, then Ruler of the world — the Father of all things. In driving away the darkness, and likewise in fertilizing the earth, the Sun becomes the preserver and kind protector of all living things—the Saviour of mankind. As the Sun sometimes scorches and withers vegetation and dries up the rivers, he was conceived of as a Destroyer also. As Creator, Preserver, and Destroyer the Sun was three persons in one — the *Trinity*.

It is very hard for man at the present day to realize the feelings with which the first dwellers on earth looked upon the Sun. "Think of man," says Professor Müller, "at the dawn of time. . . . Was not the sunrise to him the first wonder, the first beginning to him of all reflection, all thought, all philosophy? Was it not to him the first revelation, the first beginning of all trust, of all religion?"

The Aryans looked up to the sky and gave it the name of Dyaus, from a root-word which means *to shine*; When, out of the forces and forms of nature, they fashioned other gods, this name of Dyaus became Dyaus Pitar, — the Heaven-Father, or All-Father. The earth they worshipped as the Mother of All.

They said that the Sun was the Son of the Sky, or the Heaven-Father, and that the immaculate virgin, the Earth (sometimes it was the dawn or the night), was the Mother of the Sun. Hence we have the Virgin, or Virgo, as one of the signs of the zodiac.

As the Sun begins its apparent annual northward journey on the twenty-fifth of December, this day was said to be his birthday, and was observed with great rejoicings. On this day the sign of the Virgin is rising on the eastern horizon, the Sun having reached the winter solstice.

The division of the first decan of the Virgin represents a beautiful immaculate virgin with flowing hair, sitting in a chair, with two ears of corn in her hand, and suckling an infant called Iesus (Jesus in Latin), by some nations, and Christ in Greek (from the Greek Christos, — an Anointed One, a Messiah). This infant denotes the Sun, which at the moment of the winter solstice, precisely when the Persian magi drew the horoscope of the new year, was placed on the bosom of the Virgin. (See APPENDIX A.)

The zodiacal sign of Aries was anciently known as the Lamb; consequently, when the Sun made the transit of the equinox under this sign, it was called the Lamb of God.

The birth of the Sun was said to be heralded by a star — the Morning-star, which rises immediately before the Virgin and her Child. As the Sun appears to start from a dark abode, it was said that he was born in a cave, or dungeon, and the splendor of the morning sky was said to be the halo around his cradle. As the Sun scatters the darkness, it was said that he would be the destroyer of the reigning monarch, Night. Warned of this peril by oracles, Night tries to prevent the birth of the Sun, and, failing in that, seeks to take his life. For this reason it is said that the Sun is left on the bare hillside to perish, as he seemingly rests on the earth at his rising. He meets with temptations on his course, is beset by foes, clouds of storm and darkness; but, in the struggle which ensues, he is conqueror, the gloomy army, broken and rent, is scattered. The daughters of his foes, the last light vapors which float in the heavens, try in vain to clasp and retain him, but he disengages himself from their embraces; and, as he repulses them, they writhe, lose their form and vanish. Temptations to sloth and luxury are offered him in vain; he has work to do, and nothing can stay him from doing it. He travels over many lands, and toils for the benefit of others; he does hard service for a mean and cruel generation. He is constantly in company with his Twelve Apostles — the twelve signs of the zodiac.

As he approaches midsummer, he appears in all his splendor, he has reached the summit of his career; henceforth his power diminishes, and he meets with an early and a violent death, from which there is no escape. When the extreme southern limit of his course is reached, his enemies — darkness and cold, which have sought in vain to wound him — win the victory. The bright Sun of summer is slain, crucified in the heavens, and pierced by the spear (thorn, or arrow) of winter. He who has performed such marvellous miracles, healing the sick and raising the dead, cannot save himself; a stern fate decrees that he must die an ignominious death.

As the Sun wakens the earth to life after the long sleep of winter is passed, it was said that he raised the dead. He is crucified, with outstretched arms in the heavens,—outstretched to bless the world he is trying to save from the terror of darkness,—to the tree, or cross. It was an ancient custom to use trees as gibbets for crucifixion, or, if artificial, to call the cross a *tree*, the tree being one of the symbols of nature-worship, which denoted the fructifying power of the Sun. The Sun crucified was the Sun in winter, when his fructifying power is gone.

Before the Sun dies he sees all his disciples — his retinue of light, the twelve hours of the day or the twelve months of the year — disappear in the sanguinary *mêlée* of the clouds of evening; but the tender mother and the fair maidens he has loved — the beautiful lights which flush the eastern sky as the Sun sinks in the west — remain with him till the last. Their tears are the tears of dew. At his death there is darkness over all the land. He descends into Hell, or Hades. In ancient times Hell, or Hades, was a place neither of reward nor punishment, but was simply the home of the dead, good and bad alike, the word primarily signifying nothing more than the hollow grave, hole, pit, cavern, or other receptacle which receives the dead. By the Aryans, Hades was supposed to be in the far west, which to them was always the region of darkness and death, as the east was of light and life. On the twenty-second of December the Sun enters the sign Capricornus, or the Goat, and appears to remain in the same place for three days and three nights, and then begins to ascend. This was said to be the resurrection of the Sun from Hades or the grave. At the vernal equinox, at Easter, the Sun has been below the equator and suddenly rises above it. It rises triumphant over the powers of darkness and cold. The resurrection of the Sun was generally celebrated on the twenty-fifth of March, when the return of spring may be said to be the result of the return of the Sun, from the lower or far-off regions to which it had departed.

There were numerous symbols which were held as sacred to the Sun, the most common being the fish, the lamb, the cross, and the serpent. The Serpent was an emblem of the Sun, when represented with his tail in his mouth, thus forming a circle. He was an emblem of eternity, when represented as casting off his skin; but when represented with his deadly sting, he was an emblem of evil. When represented as crucified on the tree (cross), the Serpent denoted the Sun in winter, when it has lost its fructifying power.

The Aryans observed various rites and ceremonies, among them being Baptism and the sacrament of the Eucharist. Indeed, the doctrine of Transubstantiation is one of the most ancient of doctrines. Baptism was held to be a regenerating rite; and rivers, as sources of fertility and purification, were at an early date invested with a sacred character. Every great river was supposed to be permeated with the divine essence, and its waters held to cleanse from moral guilt and contamination.

The doctrines of Original Sin and the Fallen Condition of Man were not unknown to the primitive Aryan, who, in order to propitiate his gods, atone for sins, or avert calamities, offered sacrifices to them. When men lived mostly on vegetables, they offered grain, salt, fruits, water, and flowers; but when they began to eat meat and spices, and drink wine, they offered these also, — naturally supposing that the gods would be pleased with whatever was useful or agreeable to men.

In the course of time it began to be imagined that the gods demanded something more sacred as offerings, or atonements, for sin. This led to the sacrifice of human beings, at first of slaves and those taken in war, and finally of their own children, even their most beloved and first-born. It came to be an idea that every sin must have its prescribed amount of punishment, and that the gods would accept the life of one person in atonement for the sins of others. From this arose a belief in the redemption from sin by the sufferings of a Divine Incarnation, by death on the cross, or otherwise.

Branches of the Aryan race migrated to the east and to the west. One of the offshoots, at the west, founded the Persian kingdom; another built Athens and Lacedæmon, and became the Greek nation; a third went on to Italy, and reared the city on the seven hills, which grew into imperial Rome. A distant colony of the same race excavated the silver mines of prehistoric Spain; and the first glimpse at ancient England reveals Aryan descendants fishing in willow canoes. Germany also was peopled by the Aryans. Meanwhile other bands of Aryans had gone forth, from the primitive home in Central Asia, to the seacoast. Powerful bands found their way through the passes of the Himâlayas into the Punjab, and spread themselves, chiefly as Brahmans and Rajputs, over India.

Wherever the Aryans went, the sun-myths went with them, and appeared in the course of time, after their origin was forgotten, as the groundwork of religions, epic poems, folk-lore, and nursery tales. Out of these myths were shaped by degrees innumerable gods and demons of the Hindoos; the devs and jins of the Persians; the great gods, the minor deities, the nymphs and fauns and satyrs, of Greek mythology and poetry; the stormy divinities, the giants and trolls, of the cold and rugged north; the dwarfs of German forests; the elves who dance merrily in the moonlight of an English summer; the "good people" who play mischievous tricks upon stray peasants among the Irish hills; fairies and gods and heroes.

Almost all that we have of legend comes to us from our Aryan forefathers — sometimes scarcely changed, sometimes so altered that the links between the old and new have to be puzzled out; but all these myths and traditions, when we come to know the meaning of them, take us back to the time when the Aryans dwelt together in the high lands of Central Asia; and they all mean the same things

— that is, the relation between the Sun and the earth, the succession of day and night, of summer and winter, of storm and calm, of cloud and tempest, of golden sunshine and bright blue sky.

A few of the Aryan nations have preserved in their ancient poetry some remnants of the natural awe with which the earlier dwellers on the earth saw the brilliant sun "slowly rise from out the darkness of the night, raising itself by its own might higher and higher, till it stood triumphant on the arch of heaven, and then descended and sank down in its fiery glory, into the dark abyss of the heaving and hissing sea." One of these nations is the Hindoo. In the hymns of the Veda the poet still wonders whether the Sun will rise again; and asks how he can climb the vault of heaven, why he does not fall back, why there is no dust on his path.

It is to these Vedic hymns — written, it is said, from one thousand to fifteen hundred years before the Christian era — that we must go for the development which changes the Sun from a mere luminary into a Creator, Preserver, Ruler, and Rewarder of the world — in fact, into a Divine or Supreme Being. These hymns contain the germ-story of the Virgin-born God and Saviour, the great benefactor of mankind, who is finally put to death, and rises again to life and immortality on the third day.

In the Sanskrit Dictionary, compiled more than two thousand years ago, we find a full account of the incarnate deity Vishnu, who appeared in human form as Crishna. Vishnu, being moved to relieve the earth of her load of misery and sin, came down from heaven, and was born of the virgin Devaki, on the twenty-fifth of December. (See NOTE 1.)

His birth was announced in the heavens by his star, and a chorus of Devatas celebrated, with song, the praise of Devaki. "The spirits and nymphs of heaven danced and sang; and at midnight, when the Support of All was born, the clouds emitted low, pleasing sounds, and poured down rain of flowers."

Though of royal descent (he was of the Yadava line, the oldest and noblest of India) he was born in a cave, his mother being on a journey with his foster-father, on their way to the city, to pay his yearly tribute or tax to the king.

At Crishna's birth the cave was brilliantly illuminated, and the faces of his father and mother emitted rays of glory.

The divine child was recognized by cowherds, who prostrated themselves before him. He was received with divine honors, and presented with gifts of sandal-wood and perfumes. Soon after his birth he was visited by the holy prophet Nared, who had heard of the fame of the infant. Nared examined the stars, and declared Crishna to be of celestial descent.

Crishna's foster-father was warned by a heavenly voice to fly with the child to Gokul, across the River Jumna, as the reigning monarch, Kansa, sought his life. When the River Jumna was reached, the waters respectfully retired on each side, to make way for the transportation of the child. On the most ancient Hindoo temples are sculptured representations of the flight at midnight, with the infant saviour Crishna.

In order to destroy Crishna, Kansa ordered the massacre of all the male infants born in his realm during the night on which Crishna was born. The story of the slaughtered infants is the subject of an immense sculpture in the cave-temple of Elephanta. The flat roof of this cavern-temple, and every other circumstance connected with it, proves that its origin must be referred to a very remote epoch, hundreds of years before our era.

Crishna was preceded by Rama, who was born a short time before his birth and whose life was also sought by Kansa.

It is said that Crishna astonished his teachers by his precocious wisdom. Various miracles are related as occurring in his childhood, some of them being similar to those related of the childhood of Jesus Christ in the Apocryphal New Testament.

One of Crishna's first miracles, in his maturity, was the healing of a leper. He restored the maimed, the deaf, and the blind; he healed the sick and raised the dead; he supported the weak against the strong, and the oppressed against the powerful. The Hindoo sacred books teem with accounts of the miracles he performed. The people crowded his path and adored him as a god.

He had twelve favorite disciples who accompanied him on his missionary travels.

At one time a poor lame woman came with a vessel filled with spices, sweet-scented oils, sandalwood, saffron, civet, and other perfumes, and, making a sign on Crishna's forehead, poured the contents of the vessel upon his head.

He was in constant strife with the Evil One in the early part of his ministry; but he overcame the Tempter, and is represented as bruising the head of the serpent and standing upon him.

"He was the meekest and best-tempered of beings." "He preached very nobly and sublimely. He was pure and chaste in reality; and, as a lesson of humility, he even condescended to wash the feet of the Brahmans."

Crishna had a beloved disciple, Arjuna, before whom he was transfigured, and to whom he said: "Whate'er thou dost perform, whate'er thou eatest, whate'er thou givest to the poor, whate'er thou offerest in sacrifice, whate'er thou doest as an act of holy presence, do all as if to me, O Arjuna. I am the great Sage, without beginning; I am the Ruler and the All-sustainer."

Again he said: "Then be not sorrowful; from all thy sins I will deliver thee. Think thou on me, have faith in me, adore and worship me, and join thyself in meditation to me; thus shalt thou come to me, O Arjuna; thus shalt thou rise to my supreme abode, where neither sun nor moon hath need to shine, for know that all the lustre they possess is mine." "I am the cause of the whole universe; through me it is created and dissolved; on me all things within it hang and suspend, like pearls upon a string." "I am the light in the sun and moon, far, far beyond the darkness. I am the brilliancy in flame, the radiance in all that's radiant, and the light of lights." "I am the sustainer of the world, its friend and Lord; I am its way and refuge." "I am the Goodness of the good; I am Beginning, Middle, End, Eternal Time, the Birth, the Death of All."

Crishna was crucified, and is represented with arms extended, hanging on a cross, the nail-prints being visible in hands and feet, and with the spear-wound in his side. One account speaks of him as having been shot in the foot with an arrow, by a hunter, who afterwards says to him: "Have pity upon me, who am consumed by my crime, for thou art able to consume me." Crishna replies: "Fear not thou in the least. Go, hunter, through my favor, to heaven, the abode of the gods."

Crishna descended into Hell. In three days he rose from the dead and ascended bodily into heaven. All men saw him, and exclaimed, "Lo! Crishna's soul ascends his native skies!"

At his death there came calamities and omens of every kind. A black circle surrounded the moon, the sun was darkened at noonday; the sky rained fire and ashes; flames burned dusky and livid; demons committed depredations on earth; at sunrise and sunset thousands of figures were seen skirmishing in the sky, and spirits were observed on all sides.

Crishna was the second person in the Hindoo Trinity, "the very supreme Brahma; though it be a mystery how the Supreme should assume the form of man."

Vishnu is to come again on earth, in the latter days, and will appear as an armed warrior, riding a winged white horse. At his approach the sun and moon will be darkened, the earth will tremble, and the stars fall from the firmament. He is to be Judge of the dead, at the last day.

Devaki, the virgin mother of Crishna, was also called Aditi, which, in the *Rig-Veda*, is the name for the *Dawn*. Thus the legend is explained. Devaki is Aditi; Aditi is the Dawn; the Dawn is the Virgin Mother; and the Saviour of mankind, who is born of Aditi, is the Sun. Indra, worshipped in some parts of India as a crucified god, is represented in the Vedic hymns as the son of Dahana, who is Daphne, a personification of the dawn.

As the Sun and all the solar deities rise in the east, it is no cause of wonder that Aditi, the Dawn, came to be called the Mother of the Bright Gods, the Virgin Mother who gave Birth to the Sun, the Mother with Powerful, Terrible, with *Royal* Sons.

Statues of Crishna are to be found in the very oldest cave-temples throughout India, and it has been proved satisfactorily, on the authority of a passage of Arrian, that the worship of Crishna was practised in the time of Alexander the Great, in a temple which still remains one of the most famous in India,—that of Mathura, on the Jumna River.

Crishna was deified about the fourth century B. C., but the general outline of his history began, we are told, with the time of Homer, nine-hundred years B. C., or more than a hundred years before Isaiah is said to have lived and prophesied. From the date of the second century before our era, the story of Crishna was the subject of dramatic representations similar to those connected with the festivals held in honor of Bacchus.

The myths which crystallized around the name of Crishna are found in the very earliest Vedic literature, associated with other gods. Indeed, the Hindoos have had twenty-four Avatars, or Divine Incarnations. "Every time," as Vishnu is represented as saying in the *Bhagavad Gîtâ* (the *Song of the Most High*), "that religion is in danger and that iniquity triumphs, I issue forth for the defence of the good and the suppression of the wicked; for the establishment of justice I manifest myself from age to age." The incarnation of Vishnu is not a transitory manifestation of the deity, but the presence, at once mystic and real, of the Supreme Being in a human individual, who is both truly God and truly man; and this intimate union of the two natures is conceived of as surviving the death of the individual in whom it was realized.

Crishna had the titles of Saviour, Redeemer, Preserver, Comforter, and Mediator. He was called the Resurrection and the Life, the Lord of Lords, the Great God, the Holy One, the Good Shepherd.

The Evil One, the Serpent, or Satan, who figures so conspicuously in the sun-myths, is simply the dark and stormy cloud — the enemy of the Sun — personified, the Hindoo Rakshasas of our Aryan ancestors. The cloudy shape has assumed a thousand different forms, horrible or grotesque and ludicrous, to suit the changing fancies of the ages. The god of one nation became the devil of another.

The word *devil*, when traced to its primitive source, is found to be a name of the Supreme Being. The Aryan *Bhaga* (Persian, *Baga*), who is described in a commentary of the *Rig-Veda* as the Lord of Life, the Giver of Bread, and the Bringer of Happiness, has become the Bogie, or Bug-a-boo, or Bugbear, of nursery lore. The same name which suggests the supreme majesty of deity, to the Vedic poet, to the Persian of the time of Xerxes, and to the modern Russian, is in English associated with an ugly and ludicrous fiend.

The Hindoos held that there is a subtile, invisible body within the material body. They represent the constitution of man as consisting of three principles: the soul, the invisible body, and the material body. The invisible body they call the ghost or shade, and consider it as the material portion of the soul.

It appears that thinking men, while as yet on a low

level of culture, were deeply impressed by two groups of biological problems. In the first place: What is it that makes the difference between a living and a dead person? What causes waking, sleep, trance, disease, death? In the second place: What are those human shapes which appear in dreams and visions? "Looking at the two groups of phenomena, the ancient savage philosophers," says Edward Burnett Tylor, "practically made each help to account for the other, by combining both in a conception which we may call an apparitional-soul, a ghost-soul." To the savage, dreams possess a reality which a civilized man can scarcely appreciate. During sleep the spirit seems to desert the body; and as in dreams other localities and even other worlds appear to be visited, a part of the person seems to the savage to possess a separate existence. The savage believes the events in his dreams to be as real as those of his waking hours, and hence he naturally feels that he has a spirit which can quit the body.

The Hindoos believe in a Triune God: Brahma, the Father; Vishnu, the Son; and Siva, the Destroyer. (See Note 2.)

As man advanced in knowledge, and became aware of the fact that the Sun, although he appears to destroy, does not in reality, but reconstructs and regenerates the earth, the third person of the Trinity was said to be the Holy Spirit, and was symbolized by the dove. The second person of the Trinity came to be called the Word, — wisdom, or Logos, in the Greek.

Brahmanism from the very earliest times had its initiatory rites, which included baptism both by immersion and sprinkling. Infant baptism was practised, the sign of the cross being used, and a name being given to the child at that time. The symbols held as sacred by the Brahmans — the cross, serpent, dove, mitre, crosier, triangle, tripod, trefoil, key, fish, and sacred heart, — are now venerated by Christians, while the teachings of Brahmanism are very similar to the familiar teachings of the New Testament. The following precepts are from Mâhabhârata, an Indian epic poem, written many centuries before the Christian era: —

Conquer a man who never gives by gifts; subdue an untruthful man by truthfulness; vanquish an angry man by gentleness; and overcome the evil man by goodness.

To injure none by thought or word or deed, to give to others and be kind to all — this is the constant duty of the good. High-minded men delight in doing good, without a thought of their own interest; when they confer a benefit on others, they reckon not on favors in return.

Two men will hereafter be exalted above the heavens — the man with boundless power, who yet forbears to use it indiscreetly, and he who is not rich, and yet can give.

Just heaven is not so pleased with costly gifts, offered in hopes of future recompense, as with the merest trifle set apart from honest gains and sanctified by faith.

To curb the tongue, and moderate the speech, is held to be the hardest of all tasks. The words of him who talks too volubly have neither substance nor variety.

Even to foes, who visit us as guests, due hospitality should be displayed; the tree screens with its leaves the man who fells it.

Before infirmities creep o'er thy flesh, before decay impairs thy strength and mars the beauty of thy limbs, — before the Ender, whose charioteer is Sickness, hastes towards thee, breaks up thy fragile frame, and ends thy life, — lay up the only treasure; do good deeds; practise sobriety and self-control; amass that wealth which thieves cannot abstract, nor tyrants seize, which follows thee at death, which never wastes away nor is corrupted.

This is the sum of all true righteousness: treat others as thou wouldst thyself be treated. Do nothing to thy neighbor which hereafter thou wouldst not have thy neighbor do to thee. In causing pleasure or in giving pain, in doing good or injury to others, in granting or refusing a request, a man obtains a proper rule of action, by looking on his neighbor as himself.

Among the most ancient traditions of the Hindoos is that of the Tree of Life,—called *Sôma*, in Sanskrit,—the juice of which imparted immortality. This tree was guarded by spirits.

They had a legend of Paradise which reads as follows:—

In the sacred mountain Meru, which is perpetually clothed in the golden rays of the Sun, and whose lofty summit reaches into heaven, *no sinful man can exist. It is guarded by a dreadful dragon.* It is adorned with many celestial plants and trees, and is watered by *four rivers*, which thence separate and flow to the four chief directions.

In the Genesis account it is cherubim who guarded the Garden of Eden, and they were supposed to be angels; but we are told, by a recent writer, that the cherub is not an angel but an animal, and a mythological animal, at that. The cherub had the body of a lion, sometimes the head of another animal or of a man, and the wings of a bird. The cherub that was placed at the Garden of Eden, to keep the way of life was simply a dragon.

Origen believed aright, as it is now almost universally admitted, that the stories of the Garden of Eden, the Elysian Fields, the Garden of the Blessed,—which were the abode of the blessed, where grief and sorrow could not approach them, where plague and sickness could not touch them, —were founded on *allegory*. These abodes of delight were far away in the west, where the Sun goes down beyond the bounds of the earth. They were the Golden Islands, sailing in a sea of blue— *the burnished clouds floating in the pure ether.* In a word, *the Elysian Fields are the clouds at even-tide*, the picture being suggested by the images drawn from the phenomena of sunset and twilight.

The Hindoo legend of the Creation is that Siva, as the Supreme Being, desired to tempt Brahma (who had taken human form, and was called Swayambhura — Son of the Self-existent), and for this reason he dropped from heaven a blossom of the sacred fig-tree. Swayambhura, instigated by his wife Satarupa, endeavors to obtain this blossom, thinking its possession will render him immortal and divine; but when he has succeeded in doing so, he is cursed by Siva, and doomed to misery and degradation. The sacred Indian fig-tree is endowed by both the Brahmans and the Buddhists with mysterious significance, as the Tree of Knowledge, or Intelligence.

The Hindoos have an account of a Deluge similar to the account contained in Genesis, also an account of the Babel Confusion of Tongues.

They have a legend that corresponds to the

Hebrew account of Abraham and Isaac, and several accounts of seas and rivers being divided, as the Red Sea was said to be divided, for Moses and the Israelites to pass through.

They also had their Samson, whose name was Bala-Rama, the Strong Rama. He was worshipped at Mutra conjointly with Crishna; and the two were considered as one avatar, or incarnation of Vishnu, Vishnu being the Sun.

The Hindoo story of Saktideva, who was swallowed by a huge fish and came out unhurt, is similar to the Hebrew account of Jonah swallowed by the whale, which is undoubtedly a sun-myth, and represents the Sun being swallowed up by the earth, — as it apparently is when it sets in the west, — to be cast forth by the earth again in the morning. One of the names given to the Sun was Jona, and the earth is sometimes represented in mythology as a huge fish. The three days and three nights, mentioned in the account, represent the Sun at the winter solstice, when it is apparently stationary for that length of time in the sign Capricornus.

The Hindoo sacred writings relate many accounts of their Holy Ones being taken up alive into heaven, as the Hebrew Elisha was taken, and impressions on rocks are shown, as their footprints which last touched the earth.

Arresting the course of the Sun, as Joshua is said to have done, was a common thing among the disciples of Buddha. A holy Buddhist, by the name of Mâtanga, prevented the Sun, at his command, from rising, and bisected the moon. An Indian fable relates that the Sun stood still to hear the pious ejaculations of Arjuna, after the death of Crishna.

The Hindoos also have a fable which corresponds to the account of Pharaoh's two dreams.

The sun-myths finally came to be interwoven with the histories of eminent men, as in the case of the Sakya Prince Siddhârtha, afterwards called Buddha (the Enlightened One), who, the legend says, "left Paradise, and in mercy came down to earth, because he was filled with compassion for the sins and miseries of mankind. He sought to lead them in better paths, and took their sufferings upon himself, that he might expiate their crimes, and mitigate the punishment they must otherwise inevitably endure."

Buddha's Incarnation is said to have been accomplished through the agency of the Holy Spirit. Before his birth a heavenly messenger appeared in a dream to his virgin mother, Maha-Maya, and said: "Behold, thou shalt bring forth a son bearing the mystic signs of Buddha, a scion of royal lineage, a son of highest kings. When he shall leave his kingdom and his country to enter the state of devotion, he shall become a sacrifice for the dwellers of earth, a Buddha who to all men shall give joy and the glorious fruits of immortality." (See NOTE 3.)

The immortals of the Tusita-heaven decide that Buddha shall be born when the Flower-star makes its first appearance in the east. At his birth a host of angelic messengers descend and announce tidings of great joy: "A hero, glorious and incomparable, has been born, a saviour unto all nations of the earth." (See APPENDIX B.)

Princes and wise Brahmans appear and worship the child Buddha. The Rishi, Asita, to whom the devas had revealed the miraculous birth of Buddha, descends from his shady thicket, dirghavardana, to see the new-born child, and predicts Buddha's mission to save and enlighten the world.

The *Abhinish-Kramana Sutra* relates that the king of Maghada instructed one of his ministers to institute an inquiry, whether any inhabitant of the kingdom could possibly become powerful enough to endanger the safety of the throne. Two spies are sent out. One of them ascertains the birth of Buddha, his tribe and dwelling-place, and the promise of his future glory. He makes his report to the king, and advises him to take measures to exterminate the tribe.

Certain elders gave council to the king, saying, "Is it not time, O Monarch, that the infant should be presented in the temple?" A magnificent procession accompanied the child to the temple, composed of gods, cloud nymphs, etc.

Buddha's parents miss the boy one day; and after searching for him far and near, they find him in an assembly of rishis (sages of the past) who listen to his discourses and marvel at his understanding.

Buddha, before entering upon his mission, meets the Brahman Rudraka, a mighty preacher, who, however, offers to become his disciple. Some of Rudraka's followers secede to Buddha, but leave him when they find that he does not observe the fasts.

Buddha retires to the solitude of Uruvela, and fasts and prays in the desert till hunger forces him to leave his retreat. After his fast, Buddha takes a bath in the river Nerañjara. When he leaves the water, purified, the devas open the gates of Heaven, and cover him with a shower of fragrant flowers. During Buddha's fast in the desert, Mara, the Prince of Darkness, approaches him with promises of wealth and earthly glory. Buddha rejects his offers, by quoting passages of the Vedas. The tempter flees; angels descend and salute Buddha.

Buddha has frequent interviews with two buddhas who had preceded him. It is in the shade of the sacred fig-tree that the conversion and ordination of Buddha's first disciples take place. These disciples were previously followers of Rudraka. Before Buddha appoints a larger number of apostles, he selects five favorite disciples, one of whom is afterward styled the Pillar of the Faith; another, the Bosom Friend of Buddha. Among the followers of Buddha there is a Judas, Devadatta, who tries to destroy his master, and meets with a disgraceful death.

Buddha alludes to an interview with several

former Buddhas. Sceptics question his statement: "Only forty years ago you left your native town: how can you claim to have seen all those saints of old?" Buddha explains it by the pre-existence of his soul.

Buddha walks on the River Ganges. He heals the sick by a mere touch of his hand; and, according to Wassiljew, the *Mayana-Sutra* relates the miracle of the loaves and fishes. Buddha repeatedly has a miraculous escape from the snares of his adversaries. "But he, going through the midst of them, went his way." Once, when riding on his horse, Kantaka, his path was strewn with flowers thrown down by Devas. Buddha remains homeless and poor, and instructs his disciples to travel without money, trusting to the aid of Providence. At one time having no money to pay a boatman who refuses to carry him without pay, Buddha floats through the air across the stream.

To convert certain sceptical villagers he showed them a man walking across a deep and rapid river, without immersing his feet. A disciple had his feet hacked off by an unjust king, and Buddha cured him. At his appearance the sick were healed, the deaf cured, and the blind had their sight restored.

Even his disciples performed miracles. The brother of one of them being in imminent danger of shipwreck, in a "black storm," the fact was made known to the disciple by spirits, and he at once performed the miracle of transporting himself to the deck of the ship, when immediately the black tempest ceased. Several of Buddha's disciples received power to exorcise evil spirits. They also had the gift of speaking in foreign tongues.

Some of the followers of Buddha being imprisoned by an unjust emperor, an angel, or spirit, came and opened the prison-door, and liberated them.

It is related of one of his followers that his eye offended him, and that he plucked it out and cast it away.

One day Buddha's disciple, Ananda, after a long walk in the country, meets with a woman of the low caste of the Kândâlas, near a well, and asks her for some water. She tells him what she is, and that she must not come near him. He replies, "My sister, I ask not for thy caste or thy family; I ask only for a draught of water." She afterwards becomes a disciple of Buddha.

It is said that towards the end of his life Buddha was transfigured on Mount Pandava, in Ceylon. Suddenly a flame of light descended upon him, and encircled the crown of his head with a circle of light. His body became "glorious as a bright, golden image," and shone as the brightness of the Sun and moon. "His body was divided into three parts, from each of which a ray of light issued forth."

It is recorded, in the sacred canon of the Buddhists, that the multitude *required a sign* from Buddha, that they might believe.

Buddha delighted in representing himself as merely a link in a long chain of teachers.

He taught his disciples to hide their good deeds, and confess their sins before the world, — to love truth and hate the lie. He also taught that all men are brothers, that charity should be extended to all, even to enemies, and that the motive of all actions should be pity or love for one's neighbor. His disciples were told that they must renounce the world, give up all their riches, and embrace poverty.

In the Buddhist *Somadeva* is the following: "To give away our riches is considered the most difficult virtue in the world; he who gives away his riches is like a man who gives away his life; for our very life seems to cling to our riches. But Buddha, when his mind was moved by pity, *gave his life* like grass, for the sake of others."

Buddha is reported to have said: "I now desire to turn the wheel of the excellent law. For this purpose am I going to the city of Benares, to give light to those shrouded in darkness, and to open the gates of immortality to man."

When his career on earth was about coming to a close, he, "foreseeing the things that would happen in future times," said to his disciple Ananda: "When I am gone, you must not think there is no Buddha; the discourses I have delivered, and the precepts I have enjoined, must be my successors, or representatives, and be to you as Buddha."

Again he said: "Though the heavens were to fall

to earth, and the great world be swallowed up and pass away; though Mount Sumera were to crack to pieces, and the great ocean be dried up, yet, Ananda, be assured the words of Buddha are true."

At the death of Buddha, the earth trembled, the rocks were split and phantoms and spirits appeared. He descended to hell and preached to the spirits of the damned.

When Buddha was buried, the coverings of the body unrolled themselves, the lid of his coffin was opened by supernatural powers, and he ascended bodily to the celestial regions. Marks on the rocks of a high mountain are shown, which are believed to be the last imprint of his footsteps in this world.

He was called the Lion of the Tribe of Sakya, the King of Righteousness, the Great Physician, the God among Gods, the Only Begotten, the Word, the All-wise, the Way, the Truth, the Life, the Intercessor, the Prince of Peace, the Good Shepherd, the Light of the World, the Anointed, the Christ, the Messiah, the Saviour of the World, the Way of Life and Immortality. Indeed in Ceylon the name of Buddha has twelve thousand synonyms.

When the time came for him to depart, he told his disciples to no longer remain together, but to go out in companies, and proclaim the doctrines he had taught them, — to found schools and monasteries, build temples, and perform acts of charity, — that they might obtain merit, and gain access to the blessed abode of Nigban, which he told them he was about to enter.

The ever-faithful women were to be found at the last scene in the life of Buddha. At his death one of his disciples found the master's feet soiled and wet, and, asking the cause of it, was told that a weeping woman had embraced Gautama's feet shortly before his death, and that her tears had fallen on his feet and left the marks there.

After his death Buddha was exalted to the rank of deity. He was made equal to Brahma; Demons were powerless against his word; angels and arhats ministered unto him.

Buddha taught the efficacy of vicarious atonement; a hell of fire and ceaseless torment; the existence of a prodigious number of malevolent demons; the virtue of celibacy; the merit of seclusion and a retired life; the rejection of ancient rites and ceremonies; the utility of self-sacrifice; the vanity of earthly joys; the demerit of wealth; the depreciation of industry and the pursuit of worldly advantages; the merit of mendicancy; the merit of abandoning wife and children; love of enemies; patience, submission, and self-denial; submission to injustice and tyranny; the sinfulness of scepticism; auricular confession of sin, and the worship of saints.

Buddha's mercy is compared to a rain-cloud, which showers blessings upon the just and unjust. Earthly joys are compared to the grass which blooms to-day, and to-morrow is cast into the fire.

True believers are advised to gather treasures which neither thieves can steal nor fire and water can spoil. Ignorant teachers are likened to the blind leading the blind. The repentant sinner is described in a parable of a prodigal son, who wastes his substance in foreign countries, but at last returns to the house of his father, where, after serving as a common day-laborer, the son is pardoned, and becomes his father's chief heir.

The new religion spread extensively all over the vast continent of Hindostan; and finally, about three hundred years after Buddha's death, found an enthusiastic and powerful convert in the person of a king called Asoka. This ruler was imbued with a missionary spirit, and under his influence some eighty thousand missionaries went throughout India, and into China, Japan, Ceylon, Persia, Babylonia, Syria, Palestine, Egypt, — to that very populous and important emporium, Alexandria. Indeed, they seem to have gone into every country to which ships, caravans, and the flow of commerce gave them access.

Buddha's representative on earth is the Grand Lama, the high-priest of the Tartars, who is regarded as the vicegerent of God. The Tartars have œcumenical councils, monasteries, nunneries, the division of temples into a nave and transept, pulpits, dalmaticas, bell-ringing, incense, the censor suspended from five chains, chalices, chaplets, rosaries, chanted services, litanies, aspersions with consecrated water, priests with shaven polls and bare heads, confession of sins, prayers for the sick, extreme unction, masses and sacrifices for the dead, worship of relics, weekly and yearly fasts, feast of the Immaculate Conception, Candlemas, Baptism, the Eucharist, worship of one God in Trinity and a belief in Heaven, Hell, and Purgatory.

Buddhism is supposed to have been more extensively adopted than any other religion. For nearly two thousand four hundred years it has been the established religion of Burmah, Siam, Laos, Cambodia, Thibet, Japan, Tartary, Ceylon, Loo-Choo, and many neighboring islands, besides about two-thirds of China and a large portion of Siberia; and at the present day no inconsiderable number of the peasantry of Lapland are to be found among its adherents.

Its votaries are computed at four-hundred-millions, more than one-third of the entire population of the world, while Hindooism and Buddhism together have become the faiths of more than one-half the human race, and have spread Aryan theology and culture throughout Asia, to the utmost limits of China and Japan.

The Aryan sun-myths, as has been mentioned, went with the Aryans when they peopled Persia, and became the religion of the ancient Parsees. Mithras was the name which the Persians gave to the Sun. After ages had passed, it was utterly forgotten that Mithras was the Sun, and it was believed that he was the Only Begotten Son of God, who had come down from Heaven to be a mediator between God and man, to save men from their sins. The twenty-fifth of December was said to be the day on which this God-man was born, and it was celebrated with great rejoicings. The legend was that the wondrous infant was visited soon after his miraculous birth, by wise men called magi, who brought gifts of gold, frankincense, and myrrh. It was customary for the magi to ascend a high mountain, at early dawn on the twenty-fifth of December, and there, with their faces turned to the east, to wait anxiously for the first rays of the Sun, which they hailed with incense and prayer. The shepherds, also, were in the habit of prostrating themselves and praying to their god, the Sun. (See NOTE 4.)

Mithras was said to be the Logos, also the Anointed, or the Christ, and was called the Lamb of God. His worshippers addressed him in their litany, constantly repeating the words: *O Lamb of God! that taketh away the sins of the world, have mercy upon us. Grant us thy peace.* It was believed by the inhabitants of Persia, Asia Minor, and Armenia that Mithras had been put to death, been three days in Hell, and had risen again from the dead. In their mysteries was exhibited the body of a young man, apparently dead, who was presently restored to life. His disciples watched his sepulchre till midnight, on the twenty-fourth of March, with wailings and in darkness, when suddenly the place would be brilliantly illuminated, and the priest would cry: *Rejoice, O sacred Initiated; your God is risen. His death, his pains, his sufferings, have worked our salvation.* Mithras's symbol was a serpent.

The Mithrians had their mysterious meetings, their chapels, and their ceremony of initiation, which included Baptism and the Eucharist. The forehead of the initiate was marked, at the time of baptism, with the sign of the cross. Infants also were baptized, — for the purification of the soul, sin having been inherited, — a name being given to the child at that time. The ancient Persians believed that they were tainted with original sin, owing to the fall of their first parents, who were tempted by the Evil One, in the form of a serpent. Indeed, their legends of the Creation — of *Heden*, the original abode of man — and the River of Life, are almost identical with the account of the Creation and Garden of Eden, contained in Genesis. They had a legend of a Deluge, and also a legend that is similar to the Hebrew story of Jonah. (See APPENDIX D.)

The story of the War in Heaven was known to them; and was simply a myth, which represented the conflict between day and night, sunshine and storm.

The doctrine of the Millennium was familiar to them, — a time when, as they believed, the dead would be raised, and "the sea return again the remains of the departed." At this time the dead were to be judged before an assembled world, and the righteous separated from the wicked.

These doctrines were contained in the Zend-Avesta (the Living Word), which, judging from its language, is said by Professor Müller to be older than the cuneiform inscriptions of Cyrus (B.C. 560). The Persians believe that Zoroaster, the founder of their religion, received this Book of the Law from the Lord, in the midst of thunders and lightnings, as he prayed one day on a high mountain. While the King of Persia and the people were assembled together, Zoroaster came down from the mountain unharmed, bringing with him the Book of the Law. The points of resemblance between this account of the Persians and the later account of the Hebrew Moses, — bringing the Tables of the Law from Mount Sinai, — are very striking.

If we turn to the Egyptians, we shall find that the Aryan sun-myths became the foundation of their religion also. One of their names for the Sun was Osiris. The facts relating to the incarnation, birth, life, and death of Osiris are very similar to those in the legends of the Hindoo and Persian sun-gods. It was said that he was born on the twenty-fifth of December, and that he was the son of Seb and Neith, or Nut, whose common appellation was the Lady of the Sycamore. At the birth of Osiris a voice was heard proclaiming, "The Ruler of all the earth is born." Like other sun-gods, he met with temptations over which he triumphed, but was finally conquered by his foes. At the annual festival, in early spring, which commemorated his sufferings and tragical death, there was a species of drama, in which the particulars were exhibited with loud lamentations. His image — covered, as were those in the temple, with black veils — was carried in a procession. The Mourning Song, whose plaintive tones were noted by Herodotus, and has been compared to the Miserere sung in Rome, was followed in three days by the language of triumph. His tomb was illuminated, as is the Holy Sepulchre at Jerusalem, and for thousands of years it was the object of pious pilgrimages. (See NOTE 5.)

His worship was universal throughout Egypt, where he was gratefully regarded as the great exemplar of self-sacrifice, in giving his life for others, — as the Manifester of Good, as the Opener of Truth, — and as being full of goodness and truth. The Egyptian Book of the Dead, the oldest Bible in the world, represents him as "seeing all things, hearing all things," and "noting the good and evil deeds of men." On the most ancient Egyptian monuments he is represented as Judge of the Dead, seated on his throne of judgment, bearing a staff, and carrying the *crux ansata* (the most common form of the cross) with the St. Andrew's cross on his breast. These sculptures were contemporary with the building of the pyramids, which were built centuries before Abraham is said to have been born. Osiris was represented with the trefoil (the leaf of the Vila, or Bel-tree, which is triple in form) on his head, that being one of the ancient symbols of the *three-in-one* mystery — the Trinity. As second person of the Trinity he was called the Word. In one of the sacred books of the Egyptians occurs the following: "I know the mystery of the Divine Word; the Word of the Lord of All, which was the maker of it." "The Word is the first person after himself, — uncreated, infinite, ruling over all things that were made by him."

The monogram of Osiris is X and P in combination, and is now used as the monogram of Jesus Christ. His symbol is the serpent, which was the earliest symbol of Jesus, centuries later. Among the many hieroglyphic titles which accompany the figure of Osiris on the walls of temples and tombs are Lord of Life, Resurrected One, Eternal Ruler, Manifester of God, Full of Goodness and Truth.

There was great splendor of ritual in the Egyptian religion, including gorgeous robes, mitres, tiaras, wax tapers, processional services, and lustrations. The priests wore white surplices, and were shorn and beardless. There were also sprinklings of holy water. The rite of Baptism was observed, with the sign of the cross, and also the Eucharist, — the sacred cake being eaten after it had been consecrated by the priest, and made veritable "flesh of his flesh." The sun, moon, and five planets were each of them assigned a day of the week, the seventh day being Saturn's Day, and kept as a holy day. The Immortality of the Soul was believed in and was a very ancient doctrine; for on a monument thousands of years old is the epitaph: "May thy soul attain to the Creator of all mankind." Like the Buddhists, the ancient Egyptians were familiar with the War in Heaven myth and the Tree of Life myth.

Neith, the mother of Osiris, was worshipped as the Holy Virgin, the Great Mother, yet an Immaculate Virgin. There was a grand celebration held in her honor, called the Feast of Lamps, which has come down to the present time as Candlemas Day, or the Purification of the Virgin Mary.

Horus, another Egyptian name for the Sun, was said to have been born of the immaculate virgin Isis (the Moon), on the twenty-fifth of December. On this day the effigy of the infant Horus, lying in a manger, was exhibited amid great rejoicings. Being of royal descent, his life was sought by Typhon (darkness or night), and in consequence he was brought up secretly on the isle of Buto. Like other sun-gods, he was tempted, but was not vanquished. He is represented, in Egyptian art, as overcoming the Evil Serpent, and standing triumphantly upon him. It was said that he performed many miracles, among them the raising of the dead. He was finally slain, and descended into Hell. In three days he rose from the dead and ascended into Heaven. His death and resurrection were celebrated with great pomp. He was called the Royal Good Shepherd,

Lord of Life, Only-Begotten, Saviour, the Anointed, or the Christ; and when represented as Horus Sneb, the Redeemer. He is generally represented as an infant in the arms of his mother Isis, or sitting on her knee; and in many of these representations both the mother and child are black.—As the Sun seemingly rests on the earth at his rising, it was said that he was sitting in the lap of his mother; and as the earth is black, or dark, before the rising of the Sun, the mother and child were represented as black. (See APPENDIX E.)

The most ancient pictures and statues, in Italy and other parts of Europe, of what are supposed to be representations of the Virgin Mary and the infant Jesus, are black. The infant god in the arms of his black mother, with white eyes, teeth, and drapery, is himself perfectly black. The images are adorned with jewels, and in some cases the Virgin is crowned with a triple crown. The explanation of these early representations of the Virgin Mary and infant Jesus,—black, yet crowned and covered with jewels,—is that they are of pre-Christian origin; they are Isis and Horus,—and perhaps, in some cases, Devaki and Crishna,—baptized anew. In many parts of Italy are to be seen pictures of the Holy Family, of great antiquity, the groundwork often of gold. These pictures represent the mother, with a child on her knee, and a little boy by her side. The Lamb is generally seen in the picture. They are inscribed *Deo Soli*, and are representations of Isis and Horus.

The *Deo Soli* betrays their Pagan origin. Isis was worshipped in Europe as well as Egypt, for centuries before and after the Christian era. She was worshipped as the Virgin Mother, and styled Our Lady, Queen of Heaven, Star of the Sea, Governess, Mother of God, Intercessor. It is related that Isis, being at one time on a journey, came to the River Phœdrus, which was in a "rough air." Wishing to cross, she commanded the stream to be dried up, and it obeyed her. It was said that she healed the sick and gave sight to the blind. Pilgrimages were made to her temples, by the sick.

Isis was represented as standing on the crescent moon, with twelve stars surrounding her head; precisely as the Virgin Mary is now represented in almost every Roman Catholic Church on the continent of Europe. She was also represented with the infant Horus in her arms, enclosed in a framework of the flowers of the Egyptian bean, the sacred lotus; as the Virgin Mary was afterwards represented in mediæval art.

The sun-myth began its hold upon the Egyptians more than five-thousand years ago, when men trusted in a Risen Saviour, and confidently hoped to rise from the grave as he had risen.

The ancient Egyptians had the legend of the Tree of Life, the fruit of which enabled those who ate of it to become as gods.

The Egyptian records contain no account of a cataclysmal deluge, the land apparently never having been visited by other than the annual beneficent overflow of the Nile. Indeed, Pharaoh Khoufoucheops was building his pyramid, according to Egyptian chronicle, when the whole world was under the waters of a universal Deluge, according to Hebrew chronicle. The Egyptians have no account of the destruction of Pharaoh and his army, in the Red Sea, or of the other circumstances attending the Exodus from Egypt. We find, in Egyptian history, that at one time the land of Egypt was infected with disease; and, through the advice of the sacred scribe Phritiphantes, the king caused the infected people to be driven out of the country. The infected people were the brick-making slaves, known as the Children of Israel, who were infected with leprosy. "The most noble of them went under Cadmus and Danaus to Greece, but the greater number followed Moses, a wise and valiant leader, to Palestine."

Serapis was another Egyptian sun-god, whose followers were called *Christians* and Bishops of *Christ*.

In Grecian fable there are many saviours.

The sun-god Hercules, son of Zeus (the sky) and Alcmene, was born, like the other saviours, on the twenty-fifth of December — the triple night, as the Greeks named the winter solstice. At his birth, Zeus, the God of gods, spake from Heaven and said: "This day shall a child be born, of the race of Perseus, who shall be the mightiest of the sons of men." While an infant in his cradle, Hera, the life-long foe of Hercules, sent two serpents to strangle him, but he killed them. The position of the spheres, on the twenty-fifth of December, shows the zodiacal sign of the Serpent, aiming at, and almost touching, the Virgin, who has the child Iesus in her arms, in the constellation Virgo. (See APPENDIX F.)

Hercules was said to have been swallowed by a huge fish (in one account it is a dag), at Joppa, the place where the Hebrew Jonah was said to have been swallowed by a whale. Hercules remained in the fish three days and three nights (the winter solstice), and came out unhurt, with the exception of being shorn of his locks. The Sun is shorn of his locks by winter. An abundance of hair and a long beard are mythological attributes of the Sun, denoting its rays. (See NOTE 6.)

Many of the exploits of Hercules are similar to those accredited to the Hebrew Samson. Samson's death reminds us of Hercules, who died at the winter solstice, in the far west, where his two pillars are set up to mark his wanderings. Samson also died at the two pillars; but they were not the Pillars of the World, but those which supported a great banqueting-hall, and a feast was being held in honor of Dagon, the fish-god. The Sun was in the sign of the Waterman, when Samson, the sun-god, died. Samson was one of the names of the Sun, the name signifying the *sunny*, as well as the *strong*.

Hercules rose from the funeral pile and ascended into heaven in a cloud, amid peals of thunder. At his death, Iola (the fair-haired Dawn) again stands by his side, cheering him to the last. Then once more the face of Hercules flushed with a deep joy, and he said: "Ah, Iola, brightest of maidens, thy voice shall cheer me as I sink down in the sleep of death. I saw and loved thee in the bright *morning-time;* and now again thou hast come, *in the evening,* fair as the soft clouds which gather around the *dying Sun.*"

The black mists were spreading over the sky; but still Hercules sought to gaze on the fair face of Iola, and to comfort her in her sorrow. "Weep not, Iola," he said; "my toil is done, and now is the time of rest. I shall see thee again, in the bright land which is never trodden by the feet of Night." Then, as the dying god expired, *darkness was on the face of the earth;* from the high Heaven came down the thick cloud, and the din of the thunder crashed through the air.

Hercules was said to be self-produced, the Generator and Ruler of all things, and the Father of Time. He was called the Saviour, and the words Hercules the Saviour were engraved on ancient coins and monuments. He was also called the Only-Begotten and the Universal Word. He was said to have been re-absorbed into God.

The story of Hercules was known in the island of Thasos, by the Phœnician colony settled there, five centuries before the Greeks knew of it; yet its antiquity among the Babylonians antedates that.

He is identical with Izdubar, the Babylonian lion-killer.

The ancient Greeks had a tradition of the Islands of the Blessed, the Elysium, on the borders of the earth, abounding in every charm of life, and the Garden of the Hesperides,—the Paradise, in which grew a tree bearing the golden apples of Immortality. It was guarded by three nymphs and a serpent, or dragon, the ever-watchful Ladon. It was one of the labors of Hercules to gather some of these Apples of Life. When he arrived at the Garden, he found it guarded by a dragon. Ancient medallions represent a tree with a serpent twined around it. Hercules has gathered an apple, and near him stand the three nymphs, called the Hesperides.

The sun-god Dionysius (Bacchus), son of Zeus and the virgin Semele, daughter of Cadmus, King of Thebes, was born on the twenty-fifth of December. As he was destined to bring ruin upon Cadmus, he was, by the order of that monarch, confined in a chest and thrown into the Nile. Like Moses, he was rescued and adopted. He performed many miracles, among them being the turning of water into wine. He had a rod with which he could perform miracles, and which he could change into a serpent at pleasure. He crossed the Red Sea dry-shod, at the head of his army. He divided the waters of the rivers Orontes and Hydaspes by the touch of his rod, and passed through them dry-shod. By the same mighty wand he drew water from the rock; and wherever he went, the land flowed with wine, milk, and honey. It is said that while marching with his army in India he enjoyed the light of the Sun when the day was spent, and it was dark to others. Like Moses, Bacchus was represented as horned. He was called the Law-giver, his laws being written on *two tables of stone.* (See NOTE 7.)

It is related that on one occasion Pantheus, King of Thebes, sent his attendants to seize Bacchus — the Vagabond Leader of a Faction, as he called him. This they were unable to do, as his followers were too numerous. They succeeded, however, in capturing one of his disciples, who was led away and shut up fast in prison; but, while they were getting ready the instruments of execution, the prison doors came open of their own accord, and the chains fell from his limbs, and when they looked for him he was nowhere to be found.

Bacchus was called the Slain One, the Sin-Bearer, the Only-Begotten Son, the Saviour, and the Redeemer. His death, resurrection, and ascension were commemorated in early spring by festivals similar in character to those held by the Persians, Egyptians, Chaldeans, and others.

The Greeks had their Holy Mysteries. Their Eleusinian Mysteries, or the Sacrament of their Lord's Supper, was the most august of all their ceremonies. It was celebrated every fifth year, in honor of Ceres, the goddess of corn, who, in allegorical language, *had given them her flesh to eat;* and Bacchus, the god of wine, who, in like sense, *had given them his blood to drink.* These mysteries were accompanied with rites which were considered to be an expiation of sin. Throughout the whole ceremony the name of their God was many times repeated. His brightness, or glory, was not only exhibited to the eye, by the rays which surrounded his name (or his monogram, I. H. S.), but was made the peculiar theme of their triumphant exultation. The monogram of Bacchus, I. H. S., is now used as the monogram of Jesus Christ, and is wrongfully supposed to stand for *Jesu Hominum Salvator*, or *In Hoc Signo*.

The stories of Prometheus, Achilles, and Meleagros represent the short-lived Sun. Ixion, bound on the wheel, was the god Sol crucified in the heavens. The crucified dove, worshipped by the ancients, was none other than the crucified Sun; as it is well known that the ancients personified the Sun as female as well as male.

The ancient Etruscans worshipped a Virgin Mother and Son, the latter represented, in pictures, in the arms of his mother. This was the goddess Nutria. The goddess Cybele was another Virgin Mother, and was called Queen of Heaven and Mother of God. The *Galli*, now used in the churches of Italy, were anciently used in the worship of Cybele. They were called *Galliambus*, and were sung by her priests. Our Lady Day, or the

Day of the Blessed Virgin, of the Roman Church, was first dedicated to Cybele.

The ancient Scandinavians had a sun-god, or Saviour, Baldur the Good, son of the Al-fader, Odin or Woden (Heaven), and the virgin goddess Frigga. Baldur was slain by the sharp thorn of winter, descended into Hell, and rose again to life and immortality. The goddess Frigga was worshipped, and the night of the greatest festival of all the year — at the winter solstice — was called Mother-night.

The Scandinavians worshipped a triune God, and consecrated one day in the week to him, the day being called to the present time Odin's, or Woden's, day, which is our Wednesday. They observed the rite of Baptism. They had a legend of an Eden, or Golden Age, which lasted until the arrival of woman out of Jötunheim, the region of giants. They also had a legend of a deluge, from which only one man and his family escaped, by means of a bark. They had a legend corresponding to the Hebrew story of David and Goliath, in which their hero Thor (the Sun) throws a hammer at Hungnir, striking him in the forehead. The hammer was a cross. They also worshipped a god called Frey, who was fabled to have been killed at the winter solstice, by a boar (winter); therefore, a boar was annually offered at the great feast of Yule, now called Christmas. (See NOTE 8.)

The ancient Germans worshipped a virgin mother and child. The virgin's name was Ostâra, or

Eostre, whence comes our Easter. In ancient times this festival was preceded by a week's indulgence in all kinds of sports, called the *carne-vale*, or the farewell to animal food; and this was followed by a fast of forty days. This occurred centuries before the Christian era. (See NOTE 9.)

The ancient Druids of Britain were also sun-worshippers.

The idea of redemption through the sufferings and death of a Divine Saviour is to be found in the ancient religions of China. One of their five sacred volumes, called the Y-King, says, in speaking of Tien, the Holy One:—

The Holy One will unite in himself all the virtues of Heaven and earth. By his justice the world will be re-established in the ways of righteousness. He will labor and suffer much. He must pass the great torrent, whose waves shall enter into his soul; but he alone can offer up to the Lord a sacrifice worthy of him.

An ancient commentator says: "The *Holy One* [Tien] does not seek himself, but the good of others. He dies to save the world." Tien is always spoken of as one with God, existing with him from all eternity, "before anything was made."

Lao-kiun, the Chinese philosopher and teacher, born in 604 B. C., was said to be a divine emanation, incarnate in human form. He was said to have existed "antecedent to the birth of the elements, in the Great Absolute." "He was the original ancestor of the prime breath of life, and gave form to the heavens and the earth." He descended to earth and was born of a virgin, black in complexion, and described as "marvellous and beautiful as jasper." When his mission of benevolence was finished on earth, he ascended bodily into the Paradise above. Since then he has been worshipped as a god, and splendid temples have been erected to him. He taught the doctrine of One God, who is also a Trinity. His disciples are called Heavenly Teachers. What is now known as the Easter celebration was observed in China, and called a Festival of Gratitude to Tien. (See NOTE 10.)

The Chinese have, in their sacred books, a story of a Golden Age and a mysterious "delicious" garden, wherein grew a tree bearing "apples of immortality," guarded by a winged serpent, called a Dragon. The garden was moistened by four rivers, which flowed from a source called the Fountain of Immortality. One of the rivers was called the River of the Lamb. In this blissful abode there was no calamity, sickness, or death.

In one of the Chinese sacred volumes, called the Chi-King, it is written: —

All was subject to man at first, but a woman threw us into slavery. The wise husband raised up a bulwark of walls; but the woman, by an ambitious desire for knowledge, demolished them. Our misery did not come from Heaven, but from a woman. She lost the human race. Ah, unhappy Poo See! thou kindledst the fire that consumes us, and which is every day augmenting. Our misery has lasted many ages. The world is lost. Vice overflows all things, like a mortal poison.

The Chinese have a legend of the Sun standing still, and a legend of the Deluge. Accounts of the ascent to Heaven of holy men, without death, are found in their mythology. They believe that in the latter days there will be a millennium, and that a divine man will establish himself on earth, and everywhere restore peace and happiness. From time immemorial the Chinese have worshipped a virgin mother and child. The mother is called Shin-moo, or the Holy Mother, and is represented with rays of glory surrounding her head. Tapers are kept constantly burning before her images, which are elevated in alcoves behind the altars of their temples.

In the mythological systems of America, a virgin-born god, or saviour, was not less clearly recognized than in those of the Old World. Among the savage tribes his origin and character were, for obvious reasons, much confused; but among the more advanced nations he occupied a well-defined position.

The Mexican sun-god, or saviour, Quetzalcoatle, born in the land of Tulan in Anahuac, was the son of Tezcatlipoca, the Supreme God of the ancient

Mexicans, and the virgin Sochiquetzal, who was worshipped as the Virgin Mother, the Queen of Heaven. Tezcatlipoca was styled Xiuleticutle, an epithet signifying the Lord of Heaven. (*Xiuletl* signifies *blue;* and therefore was a name which the Mexicans gave to Heaven.)

Quetzalcoatle's birth was heralded by a star, and the Morning-star was his symbol. He taught metallurgy, agriculture, and the art of government. He was tempted by the Devil, and a forty days' fast was observed by his disciples. He was put to death by Eopuco, and died for the sins of mankind, after having been placed on a beam of wood, with his arms outstretched. He was represented in some instances as crucified in space, in the heavens, within a circle of nineteen figures, the number of the metonic cycle,— a serpent (the serpent, when represented in connection with a crucifixion, denoting evil, darkness, and winter) being in the picture. He was occasionally represented as crucified between two other victims. This denoted the three qualities, or personalities, of the Sun, as Creator, Saviour, and Reconstructor,—the Trinity. In other pictures he is crucified on a cross of Greek form, with the impressions of nails on the feet and hands, and with the body strangely covered with suns. In these pictures many of the figures have black faces, and the visage of Quetzalcoatle is strangely distorted.

At the death of Quetzalcoatle, "the Sun was darkened, and withheld her light." He descended into

Hell, and rose from the dead. His death and resurrection were celebrated in early spring, when victims were nailed to a cross and shot with an arrow.

The cross was said to be the Tree of Nutriment, or Tree of Life, — epithets applied by the Roman Catholics to the cross. The rite of Baptism was observed, and was believed to cleanse from sin. Infants were baptized, that sin, which tainted the child before the foundation of the world, might be washed away, and the child be born anew. The sacrament of the Eucharist was observed, the bread being made of corn-meal mixed with blood; which, after consecration by the priest, was given to the people as the flesh of their Saviour. (See NOTE 11.)

The Mexican idea of the Supreme God was similar to the Hebrew. Like Jehovah, Tezcatlipoca dwelt in the "midst of thick darkness." No man ever saw his face, for he appeared only as a shade. When he descended upon the Mount of Tezcatepec, darkness overshadowed the earth, while fire and water, in mingled streams, flowed beneath his feet, and from the summit. He was omnipresent and omniscient, a being of absolute perfection and perfect purity. The Mexicans paid him great reverence and adoration, and addressed him, in their prayers, as "Lord, whose servants we are."

In the annals of the Mexicans, the first woman, whose name was translated by the old Spanish writers "the woman of our flesh," is always represented as accompanied by a great male serpent, who seems to be talking to her. By the Mexicans, she is called Ysnextli, which signifies eyes blind with ashes. By sinning, she lost Paradise, her crime being the plucking of roses, called Fruta del arbal, — the fruit of the tree. They declare that they are still unable to look up to heaven on account of this fall.

The ancient Mexicans had a tradition of a deluge, from which a person corresponding to Noah was saved, with six others, in an ark, which landed on a mountain, a bird being sent out to ascertain when the waters had subsided. They also had a legend of the building of a tower, which would reach to the skies, their object being to see what was going on in Heaven, and also to have a place of refuge in case of another deluge. The gods beheld with wrath this edifice, the top of which was nearing the clouds, and they hurled fire from heaven upon it, which threw it down and killed many of the workmen. The work was then discontinued, as each family interested in the building of the tower received a language of its own, and the builders could not understand each other. The ancient Mexicans pointed to the ruins of a tower at Cholula, as evidence of the truth of their story.

The disciples of Quetzalcoatle expected his second advent. He told the inhabitants of Cholula that he would return to govern them. This tradition was deeply cherished by them; and when the Spaniards, with Cortez at their head, came to subdue the land, the Mexicans implicitly believed that Quetzalcoatle was returning, bringing his temples (the ships) with him.

The annunciation of the Virgin Sochiquetzal was the subject of a Mexican hieroglyphic. In this she is represented as receiving from the ambassador, or angel, a bunch of flowers. This brings to mind the lotus, the sacred plant of the East, which is placed in the hands of Pagan and Christian madonnas. The resurrection of Quetzalcoatle is represented in hieroglyphics. The cross was a very sacred symbol with the Mexicans.

Heaven they located in the Sun, and the blessed were permitted to revel amongst lovely clouds. There was a hell for the wicked, and a sort of "quiet limbo for those who were in no way distinguished." Amongst their prayers or invocations were the formulas:—

"Wilt thou blot us out, O Lord, forever? Is this punishment intended not for our reformation, but for our destruction?" Again: "Impart to us, out of thy great mercy, thy gifts, which we are not worthy to receive through our own merits."

"Keep peace with all." "Bear injuries with humility; God, who sees, will avenge you." These were among their maxims. Also: "Clothe the naked and feed the hungry, whatever privations it may cost thee; for, remember, their flesh is like thine." A Spanish writer remarks that the Devil had positively taught the Mexicans the same things which God had imparted to Christendom.

The Mexican temples — *teocallis*, or Houses of God — were very numerous, there being several hundreds in each of the principal cities of the kingdom. There were long processions of priests, and numerous festivals of unusual sacredness, as well as appropriate monthly and daily celebrations of worship. The great cities were divided into districts, each of which was placed under the charge of a sort of parochial clergy, who regulated every act of religion within their precincts, and who administered the rites of Confession and Absolution. The form of absolution contained, among other things, the following: —

Oh, merciful Lord, thou who knowest the secrets of all hearts, let thy forgiveness and favor descend, like the pure waters of Heaven, to wash away the stains from the soul. Thou knowest that this poor man has sinned, not from his own free will, but from the influence of the sin under which he was born.

The Mayas, of Yucatan, had a virgin-born god, corresponding entirely with Quetzalcoatle, if he was not indeed the same under another name. The Muyscas, of Colombia, had a similar god, who was the incarnation of the Great Father, whose sovereignty and paternal care he emblematized. The inhabitants of Nicaragua claimed that the son of their principal god came down to earth and instructed them. There was a corresponding character in the traditionary history of Peru. The Sun,

— the god of the Peruvians, — deploring their miserable condition, sent down his son, Manco Capac, to instruct them in religion. They believed in a Trinity. In Brazil, besides the common belief in an age of violence, during which the world was destroyed by water, there is a tradition of a supernatural being, called Zomo, whose history is similar to that of Quetzalcoatle. The semi-civilized tribes of Florida had like traditions. Among the savage tribes the same notions prevailed. (See NOTE 12.)

The Edues of the Californians taught that there is a supreme Creator, and that his son came down to earth and instructed them in religion. Finally, through hatred, the Indians killed him; but, although dead, he is incorruptible and beautiful. To him they pay adoration, as the mediatory power between earth and the Supreme Niparaga. They believed in a triune God. The Iroquois also had a beneficent being, uniting in himself the character of a god and man, who imparted to them the laws of the Great Spirit, and established their forms of government.

Among the Algonquins, and particularly among the Ojibways and other remnants of the Algonquin stock, this intermediary teacher, denominated the Great Incarnation of the Northwest, is fully recognized. He bears the name of Michabou, is represented as the first-born son of a great celestial *manitou*, or spirit, by an earthly mother, and is esteemed the friend and protector of the human race.

The ancient Chaldees believed in a celestial virgin, to whom the erring sinner could appeal. She was represented as a mother with a child in her arms. The ancient Assyrians and Babylonians worshipped a goddess-mother and son. The mother's name was Mylitta, and the son was Tammuz, or Adonis, the Saviour, who was worshipped as the Mediator. Tammuz was born on the twenty-fifth of December, and, like other sun-gods, suffered and was slain. The accounts of his death are conflicting. One, however, states that he was crucified. He descended into Hell; he rose from the dead on the third day, and ascended into Heaven. His worshippers celebrated annually, in early spring, a feast in commemoration of his death and resurrection, with the utmost display. An image, intended as the representation of their Lord, was laid on a bier and bewailed in mournful ditties; precisely as the Roman Catholics, at the present day, lament the death of Jesus, in their Good Friday mass. During the ceremony the priest murmured: "Trust ye in your Lord, for the pains which he endured our salvation have procured." This image was carried with great solemnity to a tomb. The large wound in the side was shown, just as, centuries later, the wound was displayed which Christ received from the spear-thrust. (See NOTE 13.)

After the attendants had for a long time bewailed the death of this *just person*, he was at length understood to be restored to life, — to have experienced a resurrection, signified by the readmission of light. The people then exclaimed: "Hail to the Dove! the Restorer of Light."

The worshippers of Tammuz believed in the Trinity, observed the rite of Baptism and the sacrament of the bread and wine. The symbol of the cross was honored by the ancient Babylonians, and is found on their oldest monuments.

The Chaldeans had their Memra, or Word of God, corresponding to the Greek Logos. In their oracles the doctrine of the Only-Begotten Son, I. A. O. (as Creator) is plainly taught.

The Babylonians had a myth of the Creation and Fall of Man, which is almost identical with the account contained in Genesis. As they had this account fifteen hundred years or more before the Hebrews heard of it, the account in Genesis was unquestionably taken from the Babylonians. Cuneiform inscriptions, discovered by Mr. George Smith, of the British Museum, show conclusively that the Babylonians had this myth two thousand years before the time assigned as the birth of Christ. The myth appears to be a combination of the phases of sun-worship which denoted the generating power of the Sun. (See NOTE 14.)

The Babylonians had an account of a deluge, which was very similar to the Hebrew account. This was also on the terra-cotta tablets discovered by Mr. Smith; and is supposed to be a solar myth, written, apparently, with a view to make a story fitting to the sign of the zodiac, called Aquarius. The Chaldeans were skilled astronomers, and, it is said, they asserted that whenever all the planets met in the sign Capricornus, the whole earth must be overwhelmed with a deluge of water.

The Babylonians had a legend of the Building of the Tower of Babel, which antedates the Hebrew account. A tower in Babylonia, which was evidently built for astronomical purposes, appears to have been the foundation for the legend. This was also described on the terra-cotta tablets discovered by Mr. Smith. The tower was called the Stages of the Seven Spheres; and each one of these stages was consecrated to the Sun, Moon, Saturn, Jupiter, Mars, Venus, and Mercury. Nebuchadonazar says of it, in his cylinders:—

The building, named the Stages of the Seven Spheres, which was the tower of Borsippa [Babel], had been built by a former king. He had completed forty-two cubits, but did not finish its head. From the lapse of time it had become ruined . . . Merodach, my great Lord, inclined my heart to repair the building.

There is not a word in these cylinders touching the confusion of tongues, or of anything pertaining thereto. It appears from other sources that the word Babel, which is really Bab-il (the Gate of God), was erroneously supposed to be from the root *babal — to confuse;* and hence arises the mystical explanation that Babel was a place where human speech became confused.

The ancient Babylonians had a legend, some two thousand years B.C., of a mighty man, Izdubar, who was a lion-slayer. From this legend the Hebrews probably obtained their story of Samson. The legend is without doubt a sun-myth. The Assyrians worshipped a sun-god named Sandon, who was believed to be a lion-killer, and was frequently figured as struggling with the lion, or standing upon the slain lion.

The Chaldeans had an account of one Zerban (*rich in gold*), which corresponds in many respects to the account of Abraham. The Assyrians had an account of a War in Heaven, which was like that described in the Book of Enoch and the Apocalypse.

"It seems," says Mr. George Smith, "from the indications in the inscriptions [the cuneiform], that there happened, in the interval between 2000 and 1850 B.C., a general collection [by the Babylonians] of the development of the various traditions of the Creation, Flood, Tower of Babel, and other similar legends. These legends were, however, traditions before they were committed to writing, and were common, in some form, to all the country."

The Hebrews undoubtedly became familiar with these legends of the Babylonians, during their captivity in Chaldea, and afterwards wrote them as their own history.

It is a fact, demonstrated by history, that when

one nation of antiquity came into contact with another, each adopted the other's myths without hesitation. The tendency of myths to reproduce themselves, with differences only of names and local coloring, becomes especially manifest as we peruse the legendary history of antiquity.

It is said of the ancient Hebrews, that they adopted forms, terms, ideas, and myths of other nations, with whom they came in contact, and cast them all in a peculiar Jewish religious mould.

"The opinion that the Pagan religions were corruptions of the religion of the Old Testament, once supported by men of high authority and great learning, is now," in the words of Professor Müller, " as completely surrendered, as the attempts of explaining Greek and Latin as the corruptions of Hebrew."

The Hebrew was a Semitic race, and consequently had inherited none of the Aryan myths and legends.

From the time of Moses till the time of the prophet Hezekiah, a period of seven hundred years or more, the Hebrews were idolaters, as their records show. The serpent was reverenced as the Healer of the Nation; they worshipped a bull called Apis, as did the Egyptians; they worshipped the sun, moon, stars, and all the hosts of heaven; they worshipped fire, and kept it burning on an altar, as did the Persians and other nations; they worshipped stones, revered an oak-tree, and bowed down to images; they worshipped a virgin mother and child; they worshipped Baal, Moloch, and Chemosh (names given to the sun), and offered up human sacrifices to them, after which, in some instances, they ate the victim. The Hebrews only began to abandon their gross Syrian idolatries after their Eastern captivity. Then also they began to collate the legends they had acquired, and write what they term history. It was not until this time that the dogmas about Satan, the angels Michael, Uriel, Yar, Nisan, the Rebel Angels, the Battle in Heaven, the Immortality of the Soul, and the Resurrection of the Dead, were introduced and naturalized among the Jews.

The theory that man was originally created a perfect being, and is now only a fallen and depraved remnant of his original self, must be abandoned, with the belief that the account of the creation in Genesis was not a revelation direct from God to the Hebrews.

With the abandonment of this theory, the whole Orthodox scheme must be abandoned; for upon this myth the theology of Christendom is built. The doctrines of the Inspiration of the Scriptures, the Fall of Man, his Total Depravity, the Incarnation, the Atonement, the Devil, Hell, — in fact, the entire theology of the Christian church, — fall to pieces with the inaccuracy of this story.

According to Christian dogma, the Incarnation of Christ had become necessary, on account of Sin, which was introduced into the world by the Fall of Man. These two dogmas cannot be separated. If there was no Fall, there was no need of an Atonement, and no Redeemer was required.

Jesus Christ saves men as he helps them, by his teachings and example, to live pure and upright lives.

As far as we can judge, Jesus himself did not assert that he was equal to, or a part of, the Supreme God. Indeed, whenever occasion arose, he asserted his inferiority to the Father. He made himself inferior in knowledge, when he declared, that of the day and hour of the Judgment, no man knew,— neither the angels in Heaven nor the Son,—no one except the Father. He made himself inferior in power, when he said that seats on his right hand and on his left, in the Kingdom of Heaven, were not his to give. He made himself inferior in virtue, when he desired a certain man not to address him as Good Master, for there was none good but God. The words of his prayer at Gethsemane, "all things are possible unto thee," imply that all things were not possible to himself; while its conclusion, "not what I will, but what thou wilt," indicates submission to a superior. The cry of agony, "My God! My God! why hast thou forsaken me?" would have been quite unmeaning, if the person forsaken and the person forsaking had been one and the same.

As was the case with Sakya Muni, and many others, the sun-myths were incorporated into the history of Jesus Christ.

There is much circumstantial evidence to show

that Jesus was an Essene, and that the Essenes were Buddhists. At the time of Christ's birth, the Jews were divided into three sects — the Pharisees, the Essenes, and the Sadducees, — the last only being purely Mosaic, and the first two being very like the Buddhists. That Buddhism had been planted in the dominions of the Seleucidæ and Ptolemies (Palestine belonging to the former) before the beginning of the third century B.C. is proved by a passage in the Edicts of Asoka, grandson of the famous Chandragupta, the Sandracottus of the Greeks. These edicts are engraven on a rock at Girnur, in Guzerat. The great missionary effort of Buddhism took place in the time of Asoka, about B.C. 307, and it was not likely that the west would be neglected when the eastern countries received such attention as they did. The Buddhist missionaries, without doubt, made their way to the Hebrews, who had always shown a great aptitude to adopt the faith of outsiders, and persuaded many of them to listen to the teachings of Siddhartha; but they were unable to convert them sufficiently to induce them to give up the Law of Moses. (See NOTE 15.)

The Essenes were a sect of unusual and singular piety, their exemplary virtues eliciting the unbounded admiration of even the Greeks and Romans. Severe asceticism, a rare benevolence to one another and to mankind in general, were their most striking characteristics. Their fundamental laws were, to love God and their neighbor, and do to others as they would have others do to them. They lived in communities or monasteries, and had all things in common, merely appointing a steward to manage the common bag.

They advocated celibacy, but had no law prohibiting marriage; though if any among them wedded, they were obliged to enter another class of the brotherhood. Their numbers were continually being augmented by additions from outside. When a person wished to enter the community, he was taken upon trial; and, if approved, he was obliged to take an oath that he would fear God and be just towards all men. He sold all that he possessed, and gave the proceeds to the brotherhood. They resembled, in their habits and customs, a fraternity of monks — of a working, rather than a mendicant order. They were all upon the same level, the exercise of authority one over another being prohibited. They abhorred slavery, and called no man on earth Master, yet they served one another. When going upon missions of mercy, they provided neither silver nor gold, but depended entirely upon the hospitality of other members of the brotherhood. When going upon perilous journeys, they took weapons of defence, but repudiated offensive war. They abjured swearing. They conversed on such parts of philosophy only as concerned God and man, and conversed not at all on secular subjects before the rising of the Sun, but prayed devoutly, with their faces turned to the east. They did not lay up treasures on earth, and despised money, fame, and pleasures, as they thought these things had a tendency to enchain men to earthly enjoyments, — a peculiarly Buddhist tenet. They considered the use of ointment as defiling, which was certainly not a Hebraic doctrine. They gave thanks before and after eating; and before entering the refectory they bathed in pure water and put on white garments. They ate only enough to sustain life. They put the greatest stress upon being meek and lowly in heart, and commended the poor in spirit, those who hunger and thirst after righteousness, the merciful, the pure in heart, and the peacemaker.

The Essenes combined the healing of the body with that of the soul; and the Greek name by which they were known, Therapeutæ (Essene is the Assyrian word for Therapeutæ), signifies *healer*, or *doctor*, and designated the sect as professing to be endowed with the miraculous gift of healing, — more especially with respect to diseases of the mind. They did not offer animal sacrifices, but strove to present their bodies "a living sacrifice, holy and acceptable unto God." It was their great aim to become so pure and holy as to be temples of the Holy Spirit, and to be able to prophesy. They reverenced Moses and had respect for the Sabbath. They practised endurance as a duty, and bore all tortures with equanimity. They fully believed in a future state of existence, in which the soul, liberated from the body, mounts upwards to a Paradise where there are no storms, no cold, no intense heat, and where all are constantly refreshed by gentle ocean-breezes. Pliny tells us that the usages of the Essenes differed from those of all other nations.

It will be evident to those familiar with the Gospels that the tenets of the Essenes and the teachings of Jesus are almost identical. Jesus differed from them, however, in some respects, as any large nature is apt to differ from others. He repudiated the extremes of the Essenes. They were ascetics, but he ate and drank the good things of life. They considered themselves defiled by contact with those less holy than themselves; but he associated with publicans and sinners.

Every Jew was obliged to be a member of one of the three sects named above, and it is but natural to suppose that Jesus would have been more in sympathy with the Essenes than with the other two Jewish sects. It is a significant fact that he frequently rebuked the Sadducees and Pharisees, but never denounced the Essenes.

As we have seen, the Essenes were ascetics and celibates, while the purely Mosaic of Jews were neither. It is true that fasting is occasionally mentioned in the Old Testament, as a sign of grief or of abasement, but never as a means of gaining salvation in a future life, — for immortality was unknown to Moses and the Jews; while celibacy is everywhere spoken of in the Old Testament as a misfortune, and an abundance of wives is regarded as a proof of divine favor.

The Jews were encouraged in having a plurality of wives, but they were nowhere directed or recommended to live on charity. The Priests and Levites were not ordered to go about the country expounding or teaching the Law. Consequently, when asceticism, preaching, and celibacy began to be advocated, between the time of Antiochus and Jesus, the inference is that they were introduced from without, and by those of the only religion which inculcated them as articles of faith and practice.

It appears singular that there should be no mention of the Essenes in the New Testament, considering the fact that the other two Jewish sects were so frequently spoken of. This can only be accounted for on the ground that the multitude of references in the New Testament to a class called the Brethren, refer to the Essenes. The Essenes were a brotherhood, and knew each other as brethren, as the Free Masons, who claim descent from the Essenes, do at the present day. We are told that the disciples were first called Christians at Antioch. They must have had a name previous to that, and we know they addressed each other as brethren.

As De Quincey says: "If the Essenes were not the early Christians in disguise, then was Christianity, *as a knowledge*, taught independently of Christ, — nay, in opposition to Christ."[1] This would explain the

[1] Historical and Critical Essays, p. 116. Boston: 1853.

very singular fact that Josephus has not mentioned Christ or the early Christians. The Essenes disappeared from history shortly after the time assigned as the crucifixion of Christ, and it is supposed that they have come down in history as Christians. Eusebius, Bishop of Cæsarea, the celebrated ecclesiastical historian, considered them Christians. He says: "It is very likely that the commentaries [Scriptures] which were among them [the Essenes] were the Gospels, and the works of the apostles, and certain expositions of the ancient prophets, such as partly that Epistle unto the Hebrews and also the other Epistles of Paul do contain."[1]

Eusebius, in quoting from Philo concerning the Essenes, seems to take it for granted that they and the Christians were one and the same; and from the manner in which he writes, it would appear that it was generally understood so. He says that Philo called them "worshippers," and concludes by saying: "But whether he himself gave them this name, or whether at the beginning they were so called when as yet the name of Christians was not everywhere published, I think it not needful curiosity to sift out."[2]

Epiphanius, a Christian bishop and writer of the fourth century, in speaking of the Essenes, says: "They who believed on Christ were called Jessæi [or Essenes] before they were called Christians. They

[1] Hist. Eccl., lib. 2, ch. xvii. London: 1637.
[2] Ibid.

derived their constitution from the signification of the name 'Jesus,' which in Hebrew signifies the same as Therapeutes, that is, a saviour or physician."[1]

Godfrey Higgins says:—

The Essenes were called physicians of the soul, or Therapeutæ; being resident both in Judæa and Egypt, they probably spoke or had their sacred books in Chaldee. They were Pythagoreans, as is proved by all their forms, ceremonies, and doctrines, and they called themselves sons of Jesse. . . . If the Pythagoreans, or Conenobitæ, as they were called by Jamblicus, were Buddhists, the Essenes were Buddhists. The Essenes called *Koinobii* lived in Egypt, on the lake of Parembole or Maria, in *monasteries*. These are the very places in which we formerly found the *Gymnosophists* or *Samaneans*, or Buddhist priests, to have lived, which Gymnosophists are placed also by Ptolemy in northeastern India.

Their [the Essenes] parishes, churches, bishops, priests, deacons, festivals are all identically the same [as the Christians]. They had apostolic founders, the manners which distinguished the immediate apostles of Christ, scriptures divinely inspired, the same allegorical mode of interpreting them which has since obtained among Christians, and the same order of performing public worship. They had missionary stations or colonies of their community established in Rome, Corinth, Galatia, Ephesus,

---

[1] Doane, Bible Myths, p. 426. New York: 1883.

Philippi, Colosse, and Thessalonica, precisely such and in the same circumstances, as were those to whom Saint Paul addressed his letters in those places. All the fine moral doctrines which are attributed to the Samaritan Nazarite, and I doubt not justly attributed to him, are to be found among the doctrines of the ascetics.[1]

In reference to this subject, Arthur Lillie says:—

It is asserted by calm thinkers like Dean Mansel, that within two generations of the time of Alexander the Great, the missionaries of Buddha made their appearance at Alexandria. This theory is confirmed in the east by the Asoka monuments, in the west by Philo. He expressly maintains the identity in creed of the higher Judaism and that of the Gymnosophists of India who abstained from the " sacrifice of living animals," — in a word, the Buddhists. It would follow from this that the priestly religions of Babylonia, Palestine, Egypt, and Greece were undermined by certain kindred mystical societies organized by Buddha's missionaries under the various names of Therapeutes, Essenes, Neo-Pythagoreans, Neo-Zoroastrians, etc. Thus Buddhism prepared the way for Christianity.[2]

We find Saint Paul, the first Apostle of the Gentiles, avowing that he was made a minister of the

[1] Anacalypsis, vol. i. p. 747, vol. ii. p. 43. London: 1827.
[2] Buddha and Early Buddhism, p. vi. London: 1881.

Gospel which had already been preached to every creature under heaven,[1] and preaching a God manifest in the flesh, who had been believed on in the world, — therefore before the commencement of his ministry, — and who could not have been Jesus of Nazareth, who had certainly not been preached at that time, nor generally believed on in the world till ages after. Saint Paul owns himself a deacon, which is the lowest ecclesiastical grade of the Therapeutan church. "The Gospel of which Paul's Epistles speak had been extensively preached and fully established before the time of Jesus by the Therapeutæ or Essenes, who believed in the doctrine of the Angel-Messiah, the Æon from heaven; the doctrine of the 'Anointed Angel,' of the man from heaven, the Creator of the world; the doctrine of the atoning sacrificial death of Jesus by the blood of his cross; the doctrine of the Messianic antetype of the Paschal lamb and of the Paschal omer, and thus of the resurrection of Jesus Christ the third day according to the Scriptures, — these doctrines of Paul can with more or less certainty be connected with the Essenes. . . . It becomes almost a certainty that Eusebius was right in surmising that Essenic writings have been used by Paul and the evangelists. Not Jesus, but Paul, is the cause of the separation of the Jews from the Christians."[2]

The very ancient and Eastern doctrine of an Angel-

[1] Colossians i. 23.
[2] Bunsen, Angel-Messiah, p. 240. London: 1867.

Messiah had been applied to Gautama-Buddha, who predicted that another Avatar would come upon earth in six hundred years after his death. This time had nearly expired; so Jesus of Nazareth was proclaimed as the expected Messiah by these Buddhist Jews, and the sun-myths were interwoven with his real history. Jesus unquestionably possessed a nature as divine as it is possible for a human being to possess, or he would not otherwise have been received as the Angel-Messiah by a sect so pure and holy as were the Essenes.

Justin Martyr, in his dialogue with Trypho, says that there exist not a people, civilized or semi-civilized, who have not offered up prayers in the name of a crucified Saviour to the Father and Creator of all things.[1]

Eusebius says that the names of Jesus and Christ were both known and honored by the ancients.[2]

The Rev. Robert Taylor, in writing upon this subject, says: —

What short of an absolute surrender of all pretence to an existence distinctive and separate from Paganism is that never-to-be-forgotten, never-to-be-overlooked, and I am sure never-to-be-answered capitulation of their [the Christians'] Melito, Bishop of Sardis, in which in an apology delivered to the emperor, Marcus Antoninus, in the year 170, he com-

---

[1] Hist. Eccl., lib. i. ch. iv.
[2] Ibid.

plains of certain annoyances and vexations which Christians were at that time subjected to, and for which he claims redress from the justice and piety of that emperor: first, on the score that none of his ancestors had ever persecuted the professors of the Christian faith; Nero and Domitian only, who had been equally hostile to their subjects of all persuasions, having been disposed to bring the Christian doctrine into hatred, and even *their* decrees had been reversed, and their rash enterprises rebuked, by the *godly* ancestors of Antoninus himself. . . . And secondly, the good bishop claims the patronage of the emperor for the Christian religion, which he calls *our philosophy*, on account of its *high antiquity*, as having been imported from countries lying beyond the limits of the Roman empire, in the reign of his ancestor Augustus, who found its importation ominous of good fortune to his government.[1]

Saint Augustine says: "That in our times is the CHRISTIAN RELIGION, which to know and follow is the most sure and certain health, called according to that name, but not according to the thing itself, of which it is the name; for the thing itself which is now called the CHRISTIAN RELIGION really was known to the ancients, nor was wanting at any time from the beginning of the human race until the time when Christ came in the flesh, from whence the true religion, which had previously existed, began to be

---

[1] Diegesis, p. 249. Boston: 1872.

called *Christian;* and this in our days is the Christian religion, not as having been wanting in former times, but as having in later times received this name." [1]

Eusebius, the great champion of Christianity, admits that "that which is called the Christian religion is neither new nor strange, but — if it be lawful to testify the truth — was known to the ancients." [2]

Ammonius Saccus (a Greek philosopher, founder of the Neoplatonic school) taught that Christianity and Paganism, when rightly understood, differ in no essential points, but had a common origin, and are really one and the same religion. [3]

Celsus, the Epicurean philosopher, wrote that "the Christian religion contains nothing but what Christians hold in common with heathen; nothing new." [4]

Justin explains this in the following manner: —

It having reached the Devil's ears that the prophets had foretold that Christ would come . . . he [the Devil] set the heathen poets to bring forward a great many who should be called sons of Jove [that is, the sons of God]; the Devil laying his scheme in this to get men to imagine that the true history of Christ

---

[1] Opera Augustini, vol. i. p. 12. Quoted in Taylor's Diegesis, p. 42.
[2] Hist. Eccl., lib. 2, ch. v.
[3] Taylor, Diegesis, p. 329.
[4] Justin, Apol. 2. See Bellamy's trans., p. 49.

was of the same character as the prodigious fables and poetic stories.[1]

Julius Firmicius says, "The Devil has his Christs."[2]

The following remarkable passage has been preserved to us by Mosheim, the ecclesiastical historian, in the life of Saint Gregory, surnamed Thaumaturgus, that is, "the wonder-worker":—

When Gregory perceived that the simple and unskilled multitude persisted in their worship of images, on account of the pleasure and sensual gratifications which they enjoyed at the Pagan festivals, he granted them a permission to indulge themselves in the like pleasures in celebrating the memory of the holy martyrs, hoping that in process of time they would return, of their own accord, to a more virtuous and regular course of life.[3]

Gregory of Nazianzus, writing to Saint Jerome, says: "A little jargon is all that is necessary to impose on the people. The less they comprehend the more they admire. Our forefathers and doctors have often said, not what they thought, but what circumstances and necessity dictated."[4]

[1] Justin, Apol. 2.
[2] Quoted in Taylor's Diegesis, p. 164.
[3] Mosheim, vol. i. cent. 2, p. 202.
[4] Hieron ad. Nep. Quoted in Volney's Ruins, p. 177, *note*. Boston: 1872.

Eusebius, who is our chief guide for the early history of the Church, confesses that he was by no means scrupulous to record the whole truth concerning the early Christians in the various works which he has left behind him.[1] Edward Gibbon, speaking of him, says:—

The gravest of the ecclesiastical historians, Eusebius himself, indirectly confesses that he has related what might redound to the glory, and that he has suppressed all that could tend to the disgrace, of religion. Such an acknowledgment will naturally excite a suspicion that a writer who has so openly violated one of the fundamental laws of history has not paid a very strict regard to the observance of the other; and the suspicion will derive additional credit from the character of Eusebius, which was less tinctured with credulity, and more practised in the arts of courts, than that of almost any of his contemporaries.[2]

Isaac de Casaubon, the great ecclesiastical scholar, says:—

It mightily affects me to see how many there were in the earliest times of the Church, who considered it as a capital exploit to lend to heavenly truth the help of their own inventions, in order that the new doctrine might be more readily received by the wise

---

[1] Eusebius, Hist. Eccl., ch. viii. p. 21.
[2] Gibbon, Rome, vol. ii. pp. 79, 80. Philadelphia: 1876.

among the Gentiles. These officious lies, they were wont to say, were devised for a good end.[1]

Cæcilius, in the Octavius of Minucius Felix, says:—

All these fragments of crack-brained opiniatry and silly solaces played off in the sweetness of song by deceitful [Pagan] poets, by you too credulous creatures [that is, the Christians] have been shamefully reformed and made over to your own god.

Faustus, writing to Saint Augustine, says:—

You have substituted your agapæ for the sacrifices of the Pagans; for their idols your martyrs, whom you serve with the very same honors. You appease the shades of the dead with wine and feasts; you celebrate the solemn festivals of the Gentiles, their calends, and their solstices; and as to their manners, those you have retained without any alteration. Nothing distinguishes you from the Pagans, except that you hold your assemblies apart from them.[2]

The learned Christian advocate, M. Turretin, in describing the state of Christianity in the fourth century, says "that it was not so much the empire that was brought over to the faith, as the faith that was

[1] Quoted in Taylor's Diegesis, p. 44.
[2] Quoted by Draper in Science and Religion, p. 48. New York: 1876.

brought over to the empire; not the Pagans who were converted to Christianity, but Christianity that was converted to Paganism." [1]

Edward Gibbon says in regard to this matter:—

It must be confessed that the ministers of the Catholic Church imitated the profane model which they were impatient to destroy. The most respectable bishops had persuaded themselves that the ignorant rustics would more cheerfully renounce the superstitions of Paganism if they found some resemblance, some compensation, in the bosom of Christianity. The religion of Constantine achieved in less than a century the final conquest of the Roman empire; but the victors themselves were insensibly subdued by the arts of their vanquished rivals.[2]

Tertullian, one of the Christian Fathers (A. D. 200), originally a Pagan, and at one time Presbyter of the Christian Church in Africa, reasons in the following manner on the evidences of Christianity:—

I find no other means to prove myself to be impudent with success, and happily a fool, than by my contempt of shame,—as, for instance, I maintain that the Son of God was born. Why am I not ashamed of maintaining such a thing? Why, but because it is itself a shameful thing. I maintain that the Son of God died. Well, that is wholly

---

[1] Taylor, Diegesis, p. 50.
[2] Gibbon, Rome, vol. iii. p. 163.

credible, because it is monstrously absurd. I maintain that after having been buried he rose again; and that I take to be manifestly true, because it was manifestly impossible.[1]

The early Christians were charged with being a sect of sun-worshippers.[2] The Emperor Hadrian could see no difference between them and the followers of the ancient Egyptian god Serapis, who was the Sun. In a letter to the Consul Servianus, the Emperor says: "There are there [in Egypt] Christians who worship Serapis, and devoted to Serapis are those who call themselves 'Bishops of Christ.'"[3]

Mr. King, in speaking of Serapis and his worshippers, says: "There is very good reason to believe that in the East the worship of Serapis was at first combined with Christianity, and gradually merged into it, with an entire change of name, *not substance*, carrying with it many of its ancient notions and rites."[4]

Again he says: "In the second century the syncretistic sects that had sprung up in Alexandria, the very hotbed of Gnosticism, found out in Serapis a prophetic type of Christ, or the Lord and Creator of all."[5]

[1] Taylor, Diegesis, p. 326.
[2] Bonwick, Egyptian Belief, p. 283.
[3] Giles, Hebrew and Christian Records, vol. ii. p. 86. London: 1877.
[4] King, Gnostics, p. 48. London: 1864.
[5] Ibid., p. 68.

In regard to the charge of sun-worship, Mr. Bonwick observes: "There were many circumstances that gave color to the accusation, since in the second century they had left the simple teaching of Jesus for a host of assimilations with surrounding Pagan myths and symbols. Still, the defence made by Tertullian, one of the Fathers of the Church, was, to say the least of it, rather obscure. 'Others,' wrote he, 'believe the sun to be our god. If this be so, we must not be ranked with the Persians; though we worship not the sun painted on a piece of linen, because in truth we have him in our own hemisphere. Lastly, this suspicion arises from hence because it is well known that we pray toward the quarter of the east.'"[1]

The Essenes always turned to the east to pray. They met once a week, and spent the night in singing hymns, etc., until the rising of the sun. They then retired to their cells, after saluting one another. Pliny says the Christians of Bithynia met before it was light, and sang hymns to Christ, as to a God. After their service they saluted one another. It is just what the Persian Magi, who were sun-worshippers, were in the habit of doing.

There are not many circumstances more striking than that of Christ being originally worshipped under the form of a lamb. The worship of the constellation Aries was the worship of the sun in his passage through that sign.[2] This constellation was called by

[1] Egyptian Belief, p. 282. London: 1878.
[2] Bible Myths, p. 503.

the ancients the Lamb, or the Ram. It was also called "the Saviour," and was said to save mankind from their sins. It was always honored with the appellation of *Dominus*, or "Lord." It was called by the ancients "the Lamb of God which taketh away the sins of the world." The devotees addressed it in their litany, constantly repeating the words, "O Lamb of God, that taketh away the sins of the world, have mercy upon us; grant us thy peace."

On an ancient medal of the Phœnicians, brought by Dr. Clark from Citium (and described in his "Travels," vol. ii. ch. xi.), this "Lamb of God" is described with the cross and rosary.

Yearly the sun-god, as the zodiacal horse (Aries), was supposed by the Vedic Aryans to die to save all flesh. Hence the practice of sacrificing horses. The "guardian spirits" of the Prince Sakya Buddha sing the following hymn: —

> Once, when thou wast the white horse,
> In pity for the sufferings of man,
> Thou didst fly across heaven to the region of the evil demons,
> To serve the happiness of mankind.
> Persecutions without end,
> Revilings and many prisons,
> Death and murder, —
> These hast thou suffered with love and patience,
> Forgiving thine executioners.[1]

Although Buddha is said to have expired peacefully at the foot of a tree, he is nevertheless described as

[1] Buddha and Early Buddhism, p. 93.

a suffering Saviour, who, when his mind was moved with pity, gave his life like grass for the sake of others.[1]

The oldest representation of Jesus Christ is a figure of a lamb,[2] to which sometimes a vase was added, into which the blood of the lamb flowed. A simple cross, which was the symbol of eternal life among the ancients, was sometimes placed alongside of the lamb. In the course of time the lamb was put on the cross, as the ancient Israelites had put the Paschal lamb centuries before. Jesus was also represented in early art as the "Good Shepherd," — that is, as a young man with a lamb on his shoulders, just as the Pagan Apollo, Mercury, and others were represented centuries before.

Early Christian art, such as the bas-reliefs on sarcophagi, gave but one solitary incident from the story of Our Lord's Passion, and that utterly divested of all circumstances of suffering. Our Lord is represented as young and beautiful, free from bonds, with no "accursed tree" on his shoulders.[3]

The crucifixion is *not* one of the subjects of early Christianity. The death of our Lord was represented by various types, but never in its actual form. The earliest instances of the crucifixion are found in illustrated manuscripts of various countries, and in ivory and enamelled images. Some of these are

[1] Max Müller, Science of Religion, p. 224. London: 1873.
[2] Jameson, Our Lord in Art, vol. ii. p. 137. London: 1864.
[3] Ibid., vol. ii. p. 317.

ascertained, by historical or by internal evidence, to have been executed in the ninth century. There is one also, of an extraordinarily rude and fantastic character, in a manuscript in the ancient library of St. Galle, which is ascertained to be of the eighth century. At all events, there seems to be no just ground at present for assigning an earlier date.[1]

Not until the pontificate of Agathon (A. D. 608) was Christ represented as a man on a cross. During the reign of Constantine Pogonatus, by the Sixth Synod of Constantinople (Canon 82) it was ordained that instead of the ancient symbol, which had been the lamb, the figure of a man nailed to a cross should be represented. All this was confirmed by Pope Adrian I.[2]

Rev. J. P. Lundy, in speaking of the fact that there are no early representations of Jesus suffering on the cross, says: "Why should a fact so well known to the heathen as the crucifixion be concealed? And yet its actual realistic representation never once occurs in the monuments of Christianity for more than six or seven centuries."[3]

The holy Father Minucius Felix, in his Octavius, written as late as A. D. 211, indignantly resents the supposition that the sign of the cross should be considered exclusively a Christian symbol; and represents his advocate of the Christian argument as retorting

[1] Jameson, Our Lord in Art, vol. ii. p. 137.
[2] Quoted in Higgins's Anacalypsis, vol. ii. p. 3.
[3] Monumental Christianity, p. 246. New York: 1876.

on an infidel opponent thus: "As for the adoration of crosses which you [Pagans] object to against us [Christians], I must tell you that we neither adore crosses nor desire them; you it is, ye Pagans, who worship wooden gods, who are the most likely people to adore wooden crosses, as being parts of the same substance as your deities. For what else are your ensigns, flags, and standards, but crosses, gilt and beautified? Your victorious trophies not only represent a cross, but a cross with a man upon it."[1]

Tertullian, a Christian Father of the second and third centuries, in writing to the Pagans, says:—

The origin of your gods is derived from figures moulded on a cross. All those rows of images on your standards are the appendages of crosses; those hangings on your standards and banners are the robes of crosses.[2]

It would appear that the crucifixion was not commonly believed in among early Christians. It is contradicted three times in the Acts of the Apostles. "Whom ye slew and hanged on a tree" (Acts v. 30), says Peter of Jesus. He states again (x. 39) "Whom they slew and hanged on a tree;" and repeats (xiii. 29), "They took him down from the tree and laid him in a sepulchre." There is no crucifixion, as commonly understood, in these statements.

[1] Taylor, Diegesis, pp. 198, 199.
[2] Bonwick, Egyptian Belief, p. 217.

Outside of the New Testament, there is no evidence whatever in book, inscription, or monument, that Jesus was either scourged or crucified under Pontius Pilate. Josephus, Tacitus, Plinius, Philo, nor any of their contemporaries, have referred to the fact of this crucifixion, or express any belief thereon. In the Jewish Talmud, Jesus is not referred to as the crucified one, but as the "hanged one."[1] Elsewhere it is narrated that he was stoned to death.[2]

Saint Irenæus (A.D. 192), one of the most celebrated, most respected, and most quoted of the Christian Fathers, tells us on the authority of his master, Polycarp, who had it from Saint John himself, and from others, that Jesus was not crucified at the time stated in the Gospels, but that he lived to be nearly fifty years old.

The following is a portion of the passage:—

As the chief part of thirty years belongs to youth, and every one will confess him to be such till the fortieth year; but from the fortieth he declines into old age, which our Lord [Jesus] having attained, he taught us the Gospel, and all the elders who, in Asia assembled with John, the disciples of the Lord testify; and as John himself had taught them. And he [John?] remained with them till the time of Trajan. And some of them saw not only John but

---

[1] Wise, The Martyrdom of Jesus of Nazareth, p. 100.
[2] Ibid., p. 106.

other Apostles, and heard the same thing from them, and bear the same testimony to this revelation.[1]

In John viii. 56, Jesus is made to say to the Jews: "Your father Abraham rejoiced to see my day; and he saw it and was glad." Then said the Jews unto him: "Thou art not yet *fifty* years old, and hast thou seen Abraham?" If Jesus was then only thirty or thereabouts, the Jews would naturally have said, "Thou art not yet *forty* years of age."

There was a tradition among the early Christians that Annas was high priest when Jesus was crucified. This is evident from the Acts (iv. 5). Now, Annas, or Annias, was not high-priest until the year 48 A. D.[2] Therefore, if Jesus was crucified at that time, he must have been about fifty years of age. It is true there was another Annas, high-priest at Jerusalem; but that was when Gratus was procurator of Judæa, some twelve or fifteen years before Pontius Pilate held the same office.[3]

According to Dio Cassius, Plutarch, Strabo, and others, there existed in the time of Herod among the Roman-Syrian heathen a widespread and deep sympathy for a "crucified King of the Jews." This was the youngest son of Aristobulus, the heroic Maccabee. In the year 43 B. C. we find this young man — Antigonus — in Palestine claiming the crown, his cause

---

[1] Quoted in Anacalypsis, vol. ii. p. 121.
[2] Josephus, Antiquities, bk. xx. ch. v. p. 2.
[3] Ibid., bk. xvii. ch. ii. p. 3.

having been declared just by Julius Cæsar. Allied with the Parthians, he maintained himself in his royal position for six years against Herod and Mark Antony. At last, after an heroic life and reign, he fell into the hands of this Roman. "Antony now gave the kingdom to a certain Herod, and having stretched Antigonus on a cross and scourged him, — a thing never done before to any other king by the Romans, — he put him to death." [1]

The fact that all prominent historians of those days mention this extraordinary occurrence, and the manner in which it was done, shows that it was considered one of Mark Antony's worst crimes, and that the sympathy with the "Crucified King" was widespread and profound.[2] Some writers think that there is a connection between this and the Gospel story; that Jesus was in a certain measure put in the place of Antigonus, just as Herod was put in the place of King Kansa, who sought to destroy Crishna.

In the first two centuries the professors of Christianity were divided into many sects; but these might all be resolved into two divisions, — one consisting of Nazarines, Ebionites, and orthodox; the other of Gnostics, under which all the remaining sects arranged themselves. The former are supposed to have believed in Jesus crucified, in the common literal acceptation of the term; the latter, — believers in Christ as an Æon, — though they admitted the

[1] Dio Cassius, bk. xlix. p. 405.
[2] The Martyrdom of Jesus of Nazareth, p. 106.

crucifixion, considered it to have been in some mystic way, perhaps what might have been called *spiritualiter*, as it is regarded in the Revelation; but, notwithstanding the different opinions they held, they all denied that the Christ did really die, in the literal acceptation of the term, on the cross. Mr. King, in speaking of the Gnostic Christians, says:—

Their chief doctrines had been held for centuries before in many of the cities in Asia Minor. There, it is probable, they first came into existence, as *Mystæ*, upon the establishment of direct intercourse with India, under the Seleucidæ and Ptolemies. The college of Essenes and Megabyzæ at Ephesus, the Ophites of Thrace, the Cretans of Crete, are all merely branches of one antique and common religion, and that originally Asiatic.[1]

Several of the texts of the Gospel histories were quoted with great plausibility by the Gnostics in support of their doctrines. The story of Jesus passing through the midst of the Jews when they were about to cast him headlong from the brow of a hill (Luke iv. 29, 30), and when they were going to stone him (John iii. 59; x. 31, 39), were not easily refuted.

There are those who consider Jesus Christ, not as a person, but as a spiritual principle, personified by the Essenes, as the ancients personified the sun, and gave to it an experience similar to their own.

[1] King, Gnostics, p. 1.

According to Josephus and Philo,[1] the Essene doctrines were kept secret with the greatest possible care. The members of the brotherhood were admitted into the assembly only after a three years' novitiate, and they were then not only sworn to secrecy, but were sworn also not to commit any portion of their doctrine to writing, except in allegory and symbolism, "as they received it;" for they were instructed only by means of allegories and symbolic representations. It was their custom to assemble and listen to interpretations of the Hebrew sacred writings from the elders among them. In regard to this practice Philo says:—

And these explanations of the Sacred Scriptures are delivered by mystic expressions in allegories; for the whole of the LAW appears to these men to resemble a living animal, and its express commandments seem to be the BODY, and the invisible meaning under and lying beneath the plain words resembles the SOUL, in which the rational soul begins most excellently to contemplate what belongs to itself, as in a mirror, beholding in these very words the exceeding beauty of the sentiments, and unfolding and explaining the symbols and bringing the secret meaning to the light of all who are able, by the light of a

---

[1] See Josephus, Antiquities, bk. ii. § 8; also Wars, bk. xviii. § 1. Philo on the Virtuous being also Free (Bohn's ed., vol. iii. pp. 523 *et seq.*), also Fragments (vol. iv.), and Essay on the Contemplative Life (vol. iv.).

slight intimation, to perceive what is unseen by what is visible.

In another place the Essenes are said "to take up the Sacred Scriptures and philosophize concerning them, investigating the allegories of their national philosophy, since they look upon their literal expressions as symbols of some secret meaning of nature, intended to be conveyed by those figurative" expressions.

They are said also to have writings of ancient men, who, having been the founders of one sect or another, have left behind them many memorials of the allegoric system of writing and explanation, and they imitate the general fashion of their sect, so that they do not occupy themselves solely in contemplation, but they likewise compose psalms and hymns to God in every kind of metre and melody imaginable.[1]

In the *Visions, Commands, and Similitudes* of *Hermas* — one of the Apocryphal New Testament books that was discarded by the Athanasian Council, but which was previously accepted by Christians — we find the Law of God spoken of as the Son of God. In the eighth *Similitude* a mystical shepherd is introduced as expounding a Vision in these words: —

This great tree which covers the plains and mountains, and all of the earth, is the LAW OF GOD, pub-

[1] Hitchcock, Christ the Spirit, pp. 34-37.

lished throughout the whole world. Now, this Law is the SON OF GOD, who is preached to all the ends of the earth. The people that stand under its shadow are those who have heard his preaching and believe, etc.

In another place (in the ninth *Similitude*) an Angel is represented as expounding a Vision, and says: "I will show thee all those things which the Spirit spake to thee under the figure of a Church. For that SPIRIT is the SON OF GOD." "In these Visions of Hermas," says Major-General Ethan A. Hitchcock, "which may possibly be a genuine Essene work, the SON OF GOD is spoken of in several ways: here, we see, as the LAW OF GOD; but manifestly not the written LAW, for that was not published to all the ends of the earth. The Spirit of the Law — that is, the Life of it — was therefore referred to; for this is 'preached' in the consciences of all men throughout the world."[1]

This would account for the fact that no hint is given in the New Testament of Christ's appearance. Mrs. Jameson, speaking on this subject, says:—

We search in vain for the lightest evidence of his [Christ's] human individual semblance, in the writings of those disciples who knew him so well. In this instance the instincts of earthly affection seem to have been mysteriously overruled. He whom all

[1] Christ the Spirit, p. 41. New York: 1861.

races were to call brother was not to be too closely associated with the particular lineaments of any one. Saint John, the beloved disciple, could lie on the breast of Jesus with all the freedom of fellowship, but not even he has left a word to indicate what manner of man was the Divine Master after the flesh. We are therefore left to imagine the expression most befitting the character of him who took upon himself our likeness, and looked at the woes and sins of mankind through the eyes of our mortality.[1]

The Rev. Mr. Geikie says, in his Life of Christ: —

No hint is given in the New Testament of Christ's appearance; and the early Church, in the absence of all guiding facts, had to fall back on imagination. In the first years the Christian Church fancied its Lord's visage and form marred more than those of other men; and that he must have had no attractions of personal beauty. Justin Martyr (A. D. 150–160) speaks of him as without beauty or attractiveness, and of mean appearance. Clement of Alexdria (A. D. 200) describes him as of an uninviting appearance, and almost repulsive. Tertullian (A. D. 200–210) says he had not even ordinary human beauty, far less heavenly. Origen (A. D. 230) went so far as to say that he was "small in body and deformed, as well as low born, and that his only beauty was in his soul and life."[2]

[1] History of Our Lord in Art, vol. i. p. 31.
[2] Geikie, Life of Christ, vol. i. p. 151.

One of the favorite ways of depicting him finally came to be under the figure of a beautiful and adorable youth, of about fifteen or eighteen years of age, beardless, with a sweet expression of countenance, and *long and abundant hair flowing over his shoulders*. His brow is sometimes encircled by a diadem or bandeau, like a young priest of the Pagan gods; that is, in fact, the favorite figure. On sculptured sarcophagi, in fresco paintings and mosaics, Christ is thus represented as a graceful youth, just as Apollo was figured by the Pagans, and as angels are represented by Christians.[1]

The following letter, addressed to the senate of Rome, is said to have been written by Publius Lentulus, Roman Procurator of Judæa in the reign of Tiberius Cæsar.

There has appeared in these days a man of extraordinary virtue, named JESUS CHRIST, who is yet living among us, and by the people, generally, accepted of as a prophet, but by some he is called the SON OF GOD. He raises the dead and cures all manner of diseases. A man tall and comely of stature, with a very reverend countenance, such as the beholders cannot but love and fear; his hair of the color of a chestnut full ripe, and plain down to his ears; but from thence downward more orient of color, waving about his shoulders. In the midst of his head goeth a seam, or partition of his hair, after

[1] J. P. Lundy, Monumental Christianity, p. 231.

the manner of the *Nazarites*; his forehead very plain and smooth, his face without spot or wrinkle, beautiful with a comely red, his nose and mouth so formed that nothing can be found fault with; his beard somewhat thick, agreeable to the hair of his head, not of any great length, but forked in the midst; of an inoffensive look; his eyes blue, clear, and quick. In reproving he is severe; in admonishing courteous and friendly; pleasant in speech, but mixed with gravity. It cannot be remembered that any have seen him laugh, but many have observed him to weep. In proportion of body well shaped, and a man for singular beauty exceeding the rest of mankind.[1]

It will be observed that the reddish, waving, abundant hair resembles the sun-gods, nearly all of them being represented with an abundance of long, waving red or yellow hair, denoting the rays of the sun.

The Imperial Russian Collection boasts of a head of Christ which is said to be very ancient. It is a fine intaglio on emerald. Mr. King says of it: "It is really a head of *Serapis*, seen in front and crowned with Persia boughs, easily mistaken for thorns, though the bushel on the head leaves no doubt as to the real personage."[2]

"There can be no doubt," says Mr. King, "that

---

[1] The Vernon Gallery of British Art, No. xxxviii.
[2] King's Gnostics, p. 137.

the head of Serapis,[1] marked as the face is by a grave and pensive majesty, supplied the first idea for the conventional portraits of the Saviour."[2]

When the temple of Serapis, at Alexandria, Egypt, was demolished by one of the Christian Emperors, there was found underneath the foundation a stone on which was engraven hieroglyphics in the form of a cross. They were said, by some of the Greeks who had been converted to Christianity, to signify "the Life to come."[3]

Clement of Alexandria assures us in his *Stromatis* that all those who entered into the temple of Serapis were obliged to wear on their persons, in a conspicuous situation, the name of *I-ha-ho* or *I-ha-hou*, which signifies *the God Eternal*. The learned Abbé Bazin tells us that the name esteemed the most sacred by the Egyptians was that which the Hebrews adopted, Y-HA-HO.[4]

It is said that when the vain Thulis appealed to Serapis, the god replied: "First God, afterward the Word, and with them the Holy Spirit."[5]

Rufinus tells us that the Egyptians are said to have the sign of the Lord's cross among those letters which are called sacerdotal, — the interpretation

---

[1] A representation of Serapis may be seen in Murray's Manual of Mythology.

[2] Gnostics, p. 68.

[3] Socrat. Hist. Eccl., v. ch. 17, also Sozomen, Hist. Eccl., vii. ch. 14.

[4] Higgins, Anacalypsis, vol. ii. p. 17.

[5] Ibid., vol. ii. p. 14.

being, "the Life to come."[1] They certainly adored the cross with profound veneration. This sacred symbol is to be found on many of their ancient monuments, some of which may be seen at the British Museum. In the London University a cross upon a Calvary is to be seen upon the breast of one of the Egyptian mummies. Many of the Egyptian images hold a cross in their hand. There is one now extant of the Egyptian Saviour, Horus, holding a cross in his hand, and he is represented as an infant on his mother's knee, with a cross on the back of the seat they occupy.[2]

The commonest of all the Egyptian crosses, the *crux ansata*, was adopted by the Christians. When the Saviour Osiris is represented holding out the *crux ansata* to a mortal, it signifies that the person to whom he presents it has put off mortality and entered on the life to come.[3]

The Greek cross and the cross of Saint Anthony are also found on Egyptian monuments. A figure of a Shari from Sir Gardner Wilkinson's book (fig. 14) has a necklace round his throat, from which depends a pectoral cross. Another Egyptian cross which is apparently intended for a Latin cross rising out of a heart, like the mediæval emblem of *cor in cruce, crux in corde*, is the hieroglyph of goodness.[4]

[1] Hist. Eccl., ii. ch. 29.
[2] R. P. Knight, Ancient Art and Mythology, p. 58.
[3] Curious Myths, p. 385.
[4] H. M. Westrop, in Gentleman's Magazine, N. s. vol. xv. p. 80.

The ancient Egyptians were in the habit of putting a cross on their sacred cakes, just as Christians of the present day on Good Friday. The plan of the chamber of some Egyptian sepulchres has the form of a cross. The cross was worn by Egyptian women as an ornament as it is worn to-day by Christians.

The ensigns and standards carried by the Persians during their wars with Alexander the Great (B. C. 335) were made in the form of a cross.[1]

Sir Robert Ker Porter, in his very valuable work entitled *Travels in Georgia, Persia, Armenia,*[2] *and Ancient Babylonia*, gives a representation of a bas-relief of very ancient antiquity, which he found at Nashi-Roustam, or the Mountain of Sepulchres. It represents a combat between two horsemen — Baharam-Gour, one of the old Persian kings, and a Tartar prince. Baharam-Gour is in the act of charging his opponent with a spear, and behind him, scarcely visible, appears an almost effaced form which must have been his standard-bearer, as the ensign is very plainly to be seen. This ensign is a cross. There is another representation of the same subject to be seen in a bas-relief, which shows the standard-bearer and his cross-ensign very plainly. This bas-relief belongs to a period when the Arsacedian kings governed Persia, which was within a century after the time of Alexander, and consequently more than two centuries B. C.[3]

---

[1] Bonwick, Egyptian Belief, p. 217. [2] Vol. i. p. 545, pl. xxi.
[3] P. 529, pl. xvi.

Sir Robert also found at this place sculptures cut in the solid rock which are in the form of crosses. These belong to the early race of Persian monarchs, whose dynasty terminated under the sword of Alexander the Great.[1] At the foot of Mount Nakshi-Rajab he also found bas-reliefs, among which were two figures carrying a cross-standard. It is coeval with the sculptures found at Nashi-Roustam, and therefore belongs to a period before Alexander's invasion.

The ancient Babylonians honored the cross as a religious symbol. It is found on their oldest monuments. Anu, a deity who stood at the head of Babylonian mythology, had a cross for his sign or symbol. It is also the symbol of the Babylonian god Bal.[2] A cross hangs on the breast of Tiglath Pileser, in the colossal tablet from Nimrood, now in the British Museum. Another king from the ruins of Nineveh wears a Maltese cross on his bosom; and another from the hall of Nisroch carries an emblematic necklace to which a Maltese cross is attached.[3] The *crux ansata* was also a sacred symbol among the Babylonians. It occurs repeatedly on their cylinders, bricks, and gems.

The cross has been honored in India from time immemorial, and was a symbol of mysterious significance in Brahminical iconography. It was the

---

[1] Pl. xvii.
[2] Egyptian Belief, p. 218.
[3] Bonomi, Nineveh and its Palaces, pp. 303, 333, 404.

symbol of the Hindoo god Agni, the *Light of the World*.[1]

It is placed by Müller in his *Glauben, Wissen, und Kunst der alten Hindus*, in the hands of Siva, Brahma, Vishnu, Yavashtri, and Jarma. Fra Paolino tells us it was used by the ancient kings of India as a sceptre.[2]

Two of the principal pagodas of India — Benares and Mathura — were erected in the forms of vast crosses.[3]

In the Jamalgiri remains and other sculptures brought to light by General Cunningham, near Peshawur, it is stated that a complete set of illustrations of the New Testament might be made, such as Mary laying her child in a manger, near which stands a mare with its foal; the young Christ disputing with the doctors in the Temple; the Saviour healing the man with a withered limb; the woman taken in adultery kneeling before Christ, whilst in the background men hold up stones menacingly. Mr. Fergusson fixes the date of the Jamalgiri monastery as somewhere between the fifth and seventh centuries, A.D.[4]

In the cave of Elephanta, over the head of the figure represented as destroying the infants, may be seen the mitre, the crosier, and the cross.[5]

[1] Monumental Christianity, p. 14.
[2] Curious Myths, p. 374. London: 1872.
[3] Maurice, Indian Antiquities, vol. 2, p. 359.
[4] Buddha and early Buddhism, p. x.
[5] Baring-Gould, Curious Myths, p. 374. London: 1872.

Mr. Doane, in his *Bible Myths* (p. 186, fig. 7), gives a representation of a pre-Christian crucifix of Asiatic origin, which is evidently intended to represent the Hindoo crucified Saviour, Crishna, the "Pardoner of Sins" and "Liberator from the Serpent of Death."[1] Plate number viii., same page, is without doubt Crishna crucified. Instead of the crown of thorns usually put on the head of the Christian Saviour it has the turreted coronet of the Ephesian Diana.

In the earlier copies of Moor's *Hindu Pantheon* are to be seen representations of Crishna (as Wittoba) with marks of holes in both feet, and in others of holes in the hands. Figure vi. has a round hole in the side. To the collar hangs the emblem of a heart.

The monk Georgius, in his *Tibetinum Alphabetum* (p. 203), has given plates of a crucified god worshipped at Nepal. These crucifixes were to be seen at the corners of roads and on eminences. He calls it the god Indra.

No sooner is Indra born than he speaks to his mother. Like Apollo and all other sun-gods, he has *golden locks*, and, like them, he is possessed of an inscrutable wisdom. He is also born of a virgin, — the Dawn. Crishna and Indra are one.[2]

---

[1] Child, Progress of Religious Ideas, vol. i. p. 72. London: 1871.

[2] Cox, Aryan Mythology, vol. i. pp. 88, 304; vol. ii. p. 131. London: 1870.

The sun-gods were generally said to speak to their mothers as soon as they were born. This myth was woven into the life of Buddha, and the *Apocryphal New Testament* makes the same statement in regard to Christ.[1]

P. Andrada la Crozius, one of the first Europeans who went to Nepal and Thibet, in speaking of the god whom they worshipped there, Indra, tells us that they said he spilt his blood for the salvation of the human race, and that he was pierced through the body with nails. He further says that, although they do not say he suffered the penalty of the cross, yet they find, nevertheless, figures of it in their books.[2]

Monsieur Guigniaut, in his *Religion de l'Antiquité*, tells us that the death of Crishna is very differently related. One tradition makes him perish on a tree, to which he was nailed by the stroke of an arrow.[3]

Dr. Inman says: "Crishna, whose history so closely resembles our Lord's, was also like him in his being crucified."[4]

On the promontory of India, in the South at Tanjore, and in the North at Oude or Ayoudia, was found the worship of the crucified god Ballaji or Wittoba. This god, who was believed to have been an incarnation of Vishnu, was represented with holes in his hands and side.[5]

---

[1] See the Gospel of the Infancy of Christ.
[2] Quoted in Higgins's Anacalypsis, vol. ii. p. 118.
[3] Ibid., vol. i. p. 144.
[4] Ancient Faiths, vol. i. p. 411. London: 1872.
[5] Higgins, Anacalypsis, vol. i. p. 147.

The cross has been an object of profound veneration among the Buddhists from the earliest times. One is the sacred *swastica*. It is seen on Buddhist zodiacs, and is one of the symbols in the Asoka inscriptions.[1] It is the sectarian mark of the Jains, and the distinctive badge of the sect of Xaca Japonieus. The Vaishnaves of India have also the same sacred sign.[2] According to Arthur Lillie, the only Christian cross in the Catacombs is this Buddhist swastica.[3]

The cross is adored by the followers of the Lama of Thibet. The Buddhists, and indeed all of the sects of India, marked their followers on the head with the sign of the cross. This ceremony was undoubtedly practiced by almost all heathen nations. The resemblance between the ancient religion of Thibet and that of the Christians has been noticed by many European travellers and missionaries, among whom may be mentioned Père Grebillon, Père Grueber, Horace de la Paon, D'Orville, and M. l'Abbé Huc.

Mr. Doane gives us a representation of the Crucified Dove worshipped by the ancients,[4] — the sun of noonday crucified in the heavens, who, in the words of Pindar (522 B.C.), "is seen writhing on his winged wheel in the highest heaven."[5]

---

[1] King, Gnostics, p. 23.
[2] Buddha and Early Buddhism, pp. 7, 9, 22.
[3] Ibid., p. 227.
[4] Bible Myths, p. 485.
[5] The Extant Odes of Pindar, translated by Ernest Myers, M.A., p. 59. London: 1874.

Says the author of a learned work, entitled *Nimrod:*

We read in Pindar of the venerable bird Iynx bound to the wheel, and of the pretended punishment of Ixion. But this rotation was really no punishment, being, as Pindar saith, *voluntary*, and prepared *by himself*, and *for himself;* or if it was, it was appointed in derision of his false pretension, whereby he gave himself out as the *crucified spirit of the world*. The four spokes represent Saint Andrew's cross, adapted to the four limbs extended, and furnish perhaps the oldest profane allusion to the crucifixion. The same cross of Saint Andrew was the *Taw* which Ezekiel commands them to mark upon the foreheads of the faithful, as appears from all Israelitish coins whereon that letter is engraved. The same idea was familiar to Lucian, who calls T the letter of crucifixion. Certainly the veneration for the cross is very ancient. Iynx, the bird of Maustic inspiration, bound to the four-legged wheel, gives the idea of *Divine Love crucified*. The wheel denotes the world, of which she is the spirit, and the cross the sacrifice made for that world.[1]

The "Divine Love," of whom Nimrod speaks, was "The First-begotten Son" of the Platonists. Plato (429 B.C.), in his *Timæus*, in philosophizing about the Son of God, says: "The next power to the Supreme God was decussated or figured in the shape of a cross on the universe."

[1] Nimrod, vol. i. p. 288; Anacalypsis, vol. i. p. 303.

This brings to mind the doctrine of certain Christian heretics (so called), who maintained that Jesus Christ was crucified in the heavens.

The crucified Iao ("Divine Love" personified) is the crucified Adonis, or Tammuz (the Jewish Adonai), the Sun, who was put to death by the wild boar of Aries, — one of the twelve signs in the zodiac. The crucifixion of "Divine Love" is often found among the Greeks. Hera or Juno, according to the Iliad, was bound with fetters and suspended in space, between heaven and earth. Ixion, Prometheus, and Apollo of Miletus were all crucified.[1]

The story of the crucifixion of Prometheus was allegorical; for Prometheus was only a title of the sun, expressing providence or foresight, wherefore his being crucified in the extremities of the earth signified originally no more than the restriction of the power of the sun during the winter months.[2]

A great number of the solar heroes, or sun-gods, are forced to endure being bound, which indicates the tied-up power of the sun in winter.[3]

Achilleus and Meleagros represent alike the short-lived sun, whose course is one of toil for others, ending in an early death, after a series of wonderful victories, alternating with periods of darkness and

---

[1] See Smith's Dictionary of Greek and Roman Biography and Mythology, under art. Hera.

[2] Knight, Ancient Art and Mythology, p. 88. New York: 1876.

[3] Goloziher, Hebrew Mythology, p. 406. London: 1877.

gloom.[1] In the tales of the Trojan war it is related of Achilleus that he expires at the Skaian, or western gates of evening. He is slain by Paris, who here appears as the Pani, or dark power, who blots out the sun from the heaven.

We have the Crucified Rose, which is illustrated in the jewel of the Rosicrucians. This jewel is formed of a transparent red stone, with a red cross on one side, and a red rose on the other; thus it is a crucified rose. "The Rossi, or Rosi-crucians, idea concerning this emblematic red cross," says Hargrave Jennings, in his *History of the Rosicrucians*, "probably came from the fable of Adonis being changed into a red rose by Venus."[2]

The emblem of the Templars is a red rose on a cross. When it can be done, it is surrounded with a glory and placed on a calvary. This is the Naurutz, Natsir, or Rose of Isuren, of Tamul, or Sharon, or the Water Rose, the Lily Padma, Pena, Lotus, crucified in the heavens for the salvation of man.[3]

The principal silver coin among the Romans, called the denarius, had on one side a personification of Rome as a warrior with a helmet, and on the reverse a chariot drawn by four horses. The driver had a cross-standard in one hand. This is a representation of a denarius of the earliest kind, which was first

---

[1] G. W. Cox, Tales of Ancient Greece, p. xxxii. London: 1870.
[2] The Rosicrucians, p. 260. London: 1879.
[3] Ibid.

coined 296 B. C.[1] The cross was used on the roll of the Roman soldiery as the sign of life. The labarum of Constantine was the X and P in combination, which was the monogram of the Egyptian Saviour Osiris, of Jupiter Ammon, and afterwards of Christ.[2] The monogram of Mercury was a cross.[3] The monogram of the Egyptian Taut was formed by three crosses.[4] The monogram of Saturn was a cross and a ram's horn; it was also a monogram of Jupiter.[5] The monogram of Venus was a cross and a circle.[6] The Phœnician Astarte, the Babylonian Bal, Freya, Holder, and Aphrodite, all had the same monogram.[7]

An oval seal of white chalcedony engraved in the *Mémoires de l'Académie royale des Inscriptions et Belles Lettres* (vol. xvi.), has as subject a standing figure between two stars, beneath which are handled crosses. About the head of the deity is the triangle, or symbol of the Trinity. This seal is supposed to be Phœnician. The Phœnicians also regarded the cross as a sacred sign. The goddess Astarte,—the moon,— the presiding divinity over the watery element, is represented on the coins of Byblos holding

---

[1] Chambers' Encyclopædia, art. Denarius.
[2] Celtic Druids, p. 127 (London: 1827), and Bonwick's Egyptian Belief, p. 218.
[3] Ibid. p. 101.
[4] Ibid. p. 101.
[5] Ibid. p. 127.
[6] Ibid. p. 127.
[7] Bonwick's Egyptian Belief, p. 218; also Cox, Aryan Mythology, vol. ii. p. 115.

a long staff surmounted by a cross, and resting her foot on the prow of a galley. The cyclopean temple at Gozzo, the island adjacent to Malta, has been supposed to be a shrine of the Phœnicians to Mylitta or Astarte. It is of cruciform shape. A superb medal of Cilicia, bearing a Phœnician legend, and struck under the Persian domination, has on one side a figure of this goddess with a *crux ansata* by her side, the lower member split.

Another form of the cross is repeated frequently and prominently on coins of Asia Minor. It occurs as the reverse of a silver coin, supposed to be of Cyprus, on several Cilician coins; it is placed beneath the throne of Baal of Tarsus, on a Phœnician coin of that town, bearing the legend, translated, "Baal Tharz." A medal with partially obliterated characters has the cross occupying the entire field of the reverse side; several, with inscriptions in unknown characters, have a ram on one side, and the cross and ring on the other; another has the sacred bull, accompanied by this symbol; others have a lion's head on obverse, and the cross and circle on the reverse.

A beautiful Cicilian medal of Camarina bears a swan and altar, and beneath the altar is one of these crosses with a ring attached to it.[1]

As in Phœnician iconography this cross generally

---

[1] These medals are engraved to accompany the articles of M. Raoul-Rochette on the Croix ansée, in the "Mémoires de l'Académie des Inscriptions et Belles Lettres," tom. xvi.

accompanies the deity, in the same manner as the handled cross is associated with the Persepolitan, Babylonish, and Egyptian gods, it is supposed that it had the same signification of "Life Eternal." It is also thought that it symbolized regeneration through water. On Babylonish cylinders it is generally employed in conjunction with the hawk or eagle, either seated on it or flying above it. This eagle is Nisroch, whose eyes are always flowing with tears for the death of Tammuz. In Greek iconography Zeus — the heaven — is accompanied by the eagle to symbolize the cloud. On several Phœnician or uncertain coins of Asia Minor the eagle and the cross go together. Therefore it is thought that the cross may symbolize life restored by rain.[1]

An inscription in Thessaly is accompanied by a calvary cross, and Greek crosses of equal arms adorn the tomb of Midas. Crosses of different shapes are common on ancient cinerary urns in Italy. These forms occur under a bed of volcanic tufa on the Albion Mount, and are of remote antiquity.

But long before the Romans, long before the Etruscans, there lived in the plains of Northern Italy a people to whom the cross was a religious symbol, the sign beneath which they laid their dead to rest, — a people of whom history tells nothing, knowing not their name, but of whom antiquarian research

---

[1] See Baring-Gould's Curious Myths of the Middle Ages, p. 363. London: 1872.

has learned this, that they lived in ignorance of the arts of civilization, that they dwelt in villages built on platforms over lakes, and that they trusted in the cross to guard, and may be to revive, their loved ones whom they committed to the dust.[1]

The ancient cemeteries of Villanova, near Bologna, and Golaseca, on the plateau of Somma, at the extremity of Lake Maggiore, show conclusively that above a thousand years before Christ the cross was already a religious emblem of frequent employment.[2]

The most ancient coins of the Gauls were circular, with a cross in the middle, like little wheels, as it were, with four large perforations. That these *rouelles* were not designed to represent wheels is apparent from there being only four spokes, placed at right angles. Moreover, when the coins of the Greek type took their place the cross was continued as the ornamentation of the coin.[3]

The reverse of the coins of the Volcæ Tectosages, who inhabited the greater portion of Languedoc, was impressed with crosses, their angles filled with pellets, so like those on the silver coins of the Edwards that, were it not for the quality of the metal, one would take these Gaulish coins to be the production of the Middle Ages. The Leuci, who inhabited the country round the modern Toul, had similar coins.

[1] Curious Myths, p. 364.
[2] De Mortillet, Le Signe de la Croix avant le Christianisme. Paris : 1866.
[3] Curious Myths, p. 348.

Near Paris, at Choisy-le-Roy, was discovered a Gaulish coin representing a head, in barbarous imitation of that on a Greek medal, and the reverse occupied by a serpent coiled round the circumference, enclosing two birds. Between these birds is a cross, with pellets at the end of each limb, and a pellet in each angle.[1]

A similar coin has been found in numbers near Arthenay, in Loiret, as well as others of analogous type. Other Gaulish coins bear the cross on both obverse and reverse. About two hundred pieces of this description were found in 1835 in the village of Cremiat-sur-Yen, near Quimper, in a brown earthen urn, with ashes and charcoal, in a rude kistvaen of stone blocks, — proving that the cross was used on the coins in Armorica at the time when incineration was practised.[2]

Just as the Saint George's cross appears on the Gaulish coins, so does the cross cramponnée, or Thor's hammer, appear on the Scandinavian moneys.

In ploughing a field near Bornholm, in Fyen, in 1835, a discovery was made of several gold coins and ornaments belonging to ancient Danish civilization. They were impressed with a four-footed horned beast, girthed and mounted by a monstrous human head, intended in barbaric fashion to represent the rider. In front of the head was the sign of Thor's hammer. Some of these specimens exhibited likewise the name of Thor in Runes.

[1] Curious Myths, p. 349.   [2] Ibid., p. 350.

King Olaf, Longfellow tells us, when keeping Christmas at Drontheim:—

> O'er his drinking-horn, the sign
> He made of the Cross Divine,
>   As he drank and muttered his prayers;
> But the Berserks evermore
> Made the sign of the Hammer of Thor,
>   Over theirs.

They both made the same symbol. This we are told by Snorro Sturleson, in the Heimskringla,[1] when he describes the sacrifice at Lade, at which King Hakon, Athelstan's foster-son, was present.

Now when the first full goblet was filled, Earl Sigurd spoke some words over it, and blessed it in Odin's name, and drank to the king out of the horn; and the king then took it and made the sign of the cross over it. Then said Kaare of Greyting, "What does the king mean by doing so? will he not sacrifice?" But Earl Sigurd replied, "The king is doing what all of you do who trust in your power and strength; for he is blessing the full goblet in the name of Thor, by making the sign of his hammer over it before he drinks it."

It was with this hammer that Thor crushed the head of the great Mitgard serpent; that he destroyed the giants; that he restored the dead goats to life which drew his car; that he consecrated the pyre of Baldur. The cross of Thor is still used in Iceland

---

[1] Heimskringla, Saga iv., c. 18 ¶ A.

as a magical sign in connection with storms of wind and rain. The German peasantry use the sign of the cross to dispel a thunder-storm, the cross being used because it resembles Thor's hammer, Thor being the Thunderer. For the same reason bells were often marked with the "fylfot," or cross of Thor, especially where the Norse settled, as in Lincolnshire and Yorkshire. Thor's cross is on the bells of Appleby, Scothern, Waddingham, Bishop's Norton, and Barkwith, also those of Hathersage in Derbyshire, Mexborough in Yorkshire, and many more.

The fylfot is the sacred swastica of the Buddhists, and the symbol of Buddha. The early Aryan nations called the cross *arani*. Its two arms were named *pramatha* and swastica. They were merely two pieces of wood with handles, and by rubbing together they kindled the sacred fire *agni*.

From pramatha comes the Grecian myth of Prometheus, who stole the fire of heaven from Zeus in a hollow staff and kindled the divine spark of life in man formed of clay. Hence in worshipping the cross, the Aryans were but worshipping the element fire.[1]

On the reverse of a coin found at Ugain is a cross of equal arms, with a circle at the extremity of each, and the fylfot in each circle.

The same peculiar figure occurs on coins of Syra-

[1] W. B. Wilson, The Cross Ancient and Modern, p. 11. New York: 1888.

cuse, Corinth, and Chalcedon, and is frequently employed on Etruscan cinerary urns. It appears on the dress of a fossor, as a sort of badge of his office, on one of the paintings in the Roman Catacombs.[1]

The cross was found among the ruins of Pompeii.[2]

In the depths of the forests of Central America is a ruined city, Palenque, founded, according to tradition, by Votan, in the ninth century before the Christian era. The principal building in Palenque is the palace. The eastern façade has fourteen doors opening on a terrace, with bas-reliefs between them. A noble tower rises above the courtyard in the centre. In this building are several small temples or chapels, with altars standing. At the back of one of these altars is a slab of gypsum, on which are sculptured two figures standing one on each side of a cross, to which one is extending his hands with an offering of a baby or a monkey. The cross is surrounded with rich feather-work and ornamental chains.

The style of sculpture and the accompanying hieroglyphic inscriptions leave no room for doubting it to be a heathen representation. Above the cross is a bird of peculiar character, perched like the eagle of Nisroch on a cross upon a Babylonish cylinder. The same cross is represented on old pre-Mexican MSS., as in the Dresden Codex, and that in the possession of Herr Fejérváry, at the end of which is a colossal cross, in the midst of which is represented

---

[1] Curious Myths, p. 354.
[2] Pentateuch Examined, vol. vi. p. 115.

a bleeding deity, and figures standing round a Tau cross, upon which is perched the sacred bird.[1]

A very fine and highly polished cross which was taken from the Incas was placed in the Roman Catholic cathedral at Cusco.[2]

The cross was used in the north of Mexico. It occurs amongst the Mixtecas and in Queredaro. Siguenza mentions an Indian cross which was found in the cave of Mixteca Baja. Among the ruins on the island of Zaputero in Lake Nicaragua were also found old crosses reverenced by the Indians. White marble crosses were found on the island of St. Ulloa, on its discovery. In the State of Ooxaca, the Spaniards found that wooden crosses were erected as sacred symbols, so also in Aguatolco, and among the Zapatecas. The cross was venerated as far as Florida on one side, and Cibola on the other. In South America the same sign was considered symbolical and sacred. It was revered in Paraguay. Among the Muyscas at Cumana the cross was regarded with devotion and was believed to be endowed with power to drive away evil spirits; consequently new-born children were placed under the sign.[3]

The cross was the central object in the great temple Cogames.

---

[1] Klemm, Kulturgeschichte, v. 142, 143.
[2] Higgins, Anacalypsis, vol. ii. p. 32.
[3] See list of authorities in Müller, Geschichte der Amerikanishen Urreligionen (Basil, 1855), pp. 371, 421, 498, 499.

Lord Kingsborough speaks of crosses being found in Mexico, Peru, and Yucatan.[1] He also informs us that the banner of Montezuma was a cross. The historical paintings of the *Codex Vaticanus* represent him carrying a banner with a cross on it.[2]

When the Spanish missionaries found that the cross was no new object to the red men, they were in doubt whether to ascribe the fact to the pious labors of Saint Thomas, whom they thought might have found his way to America, or to the subtleties of Satan.

The Toltecs asserted that their national deity introduced the sign and ritual of the cross.

Besides the cross, the Buddhist symbols of the elephant and the cobra were found in Mexico, also the figure of Buddha. Mr. Lillie, in his *Buddha and Early Buddhism*,[3] gives considerable evidence from Chinese records showing that the missionaries of Buddha evangelized America in the fifth century A. D., and persuaded King Quetzal Coatl to abolish the sacrifice of blood.

[1] Mexican Antiquities, vol. vi. pp. 165, 180.
[2] Ibid., p. 179.
[3] Buddha and Early Buddhism, ch. xv.

APPENDICES.

APPENDIX A.

AN EXPLANATION OF THE FABLE, IN WHICH THE SUN IS WORSHIPPED UNDER THE NAME OF CHRIST.

IT is a fact that at the hour of midnight on the 25th of December, in the centuries when Christianity made its appearance, the celestial sign, which rose at the horizon, and the ascendant of which presided at the opening of the new solar revolution, was the Virgin of the constellations. It is another fact, that the God Sun, born at the winter solstice, is re-united with her and surrounds her with his lustre at the time of our feast of the Assumption, or the re-union of mother and son. And still another fact is, that, when she comes out heliacally from the solar rays at that moment, we celebrate her appearance in the World, or her Nativity. It is but natural to suppose that those who personified the Sun, and who made it pass through the various ages of the human life, who imagined for it a series of wonderful adventures, sung either in poems or narrated in legends, did not fail to draw its horoscopes, the same as horoscopes were drawn for other children at the precise moment of their birth. This was especially the custom of the Chaldeans and of the Magi. Afterwards this feast was celebrated under the name of *dies natalis*, or feast of the birthday. Now, the celestial Virgin, who presided at the birth of the god Day personified, was presumed to be his mother, and thus fulfil the prophecy of the astrologer who had said, " A virgin shall conceive and bring forth"; in other words, that she shall give birth to the God Sun, like the Virgin of Saïs. From this idea are derived the pictures, which are delineated in the sphere of the Magi, of which Abulmazar has given us a description, and of which Kirker, Seldon, the famous Pic, Roger Bacon, Albert the Great, Blaën, Stoffler, and a great many others have spoken. We are extracting here the passage from Abulmazar. "We see," says Abulmazar, "in the first decan, or in the first ten degrees of the sign of the Virgin, according to the traditions of the ancient Persians, Chaldeans, Egyptians, of Hermes and of Æsculapius, a young maiden, called in the Persian language Seclenidos de Darzama, a name when translated into Arabian by that of Aderenedesa, signifies a chaste, pure, and immaculate virgin, of a handsome figure, agreeable countenance, long hair, and modest mien. She holds in her hand two ears of corn; she sits on a throne; she nourishes and suckles a babe, which some call Jesus, and the Greeks call Christ." The Persian sphere published by Scaliger as a sequel of his notes on Manilius, gives about the same description of the celestial Virgin; but there is no mention made of the child which she suckles. It places alongside of her a man, which can only be Boötes, called the foster-father of the son of the Virgin Isis, or of Horus.

The Sun is neither born nor does it die; but, in the relation which the days engendered by it have with the nights, there is in this world a progressive gradation of increase and decrease, which has originated some very ingenious fictions amongst the ancient theologians. They have assimilated this generation, this periodical increase and decrease of the day, to that of man, who, after having been born, grown up, and reached manhood, degenerates and decreases until he has finally arrived at the term of the career allotted to him by Nature to travel over. The God of Day, personified in the sacred allegories, had therefore to submit to the whole destiny of man: he had his cradle and his tomb. He was a child at the winter solstice, at the moment when the days begin to grow. Under this form they exposed his image in the ancient temples, in order to receive the homage of his worshippers; "because," says Macrobius, "the day being then the shortest, this god seems to be yet a feeble child." This is the child of the mysteries, he whose image was brought out from the recesses of their sanctuaries by the Egyptians every year on a certain day.

This is the child of which the goddess of Saïs claimed to be the mother, in that famous inscription, where these words could be read: "The fruit which I have brought forth is the Sun." This is the feeble child, born in the midst of the darkest night, of which this Virgin of Saïs was delivered about the winter solstice, according to Plutarch.

In an ancient Christian work, called the *Chronicle of Alexandria*, occurs the following: "Watch how Egypt has constructed the child birth of a virgin, and the birth of her son, who was exposed in a crib to the adoration of her people." (See *Bonwick's Egyptian Belief*, p. 143.)

The Sun being the only redeemer of the evils which winter produces, and presumed in the sacerdotal fictions to be born at the solstice, must remain yet three months more in the inferior regions, in the regions affected by evil and darkness, and there be subject to their ruler before it makes the famous passage of the vernal equinox, which assures its triumph over night, and which renews the face of the earth. They must, therefore, make him live during all that time exposed to all the infirmities of mortal life, until he has resumed the rights of divinity in his triumph. (See *Origin of All Religions*, pp. 232, 238.)

In the national library there is an Arabian manuscript containing the twelve signs, delineated and colored, in which is a young child alongside of the Virgin, being represented in about the same style as our Virgins, and like an Egyptian Isis and her son.

"In the first decade of the Virgin rises a maid, called in Arabic 'Aderenedesa' — that is, pure, immaculate virgin, — graceful in person, charming in countenance, modest in habit, with loosened hair, holding in her hand two ears of wheat, sitting upon an embroidered throne, nursing a boy, and rightly feeding him in the place called *Hebraea*. A boy I say, named Iessus by certain nations, which signifies Issa, whom they also call Christ in Greek." (Kircher, *Œdipus Ægypticus*.)

"The celestial Virgin was represented in the Indian zodiac of Sir William Jones with ears of corn in one hand and the lotus in the other. In Kircher's zodiac of Hermes she has corn in both hands. In other planispheres of the Egyptian priests she carries ears of corn in one hand, and the infant Horus in the other. In Roman Catholic countries she is generally represented with the child in one hand and the lotus, or lily, in the other. In Montfaucon's work (vol. ii.) she is represented as a female nursing a child, with ears of corn in her hand and the legend IAO. She is seated on clouds. A star is at her head. The reading of the Greek letters from right to left show this to be very ancient." (*Bible Myths*, pp. 474, 475.)

Mr. Cox tells us (*Aryan Myths*, vol. i., p. 228), that with scarcely an exception, all the names by which the Virgin goddess of the Akropolis was known, point to the mythology of the Dawn. In Grecian mythology Theseus was said to have been born of Aithra, "the pure air"; Œdipus of Iokaste, "the violet light of morning." Perseus was born of the Virgin Danaë, and was called the "Son of the bright morning." In Io, the mother of the "sacred bull," the mother also of Hercules, we see the "violet-tinted morning." We read in the *Vishnu Purana* that "The Sun of Achyuta (God, the Imperishable) rose in the dawn of Devaki, to cause the lotus petal of the universe (Crishna) to expand. On the day of his birth the quarters of the horizon were irradiate with joy," etc.

As the hour of the Sun's birth draws near, the mother becomes more beautiful, her form more brilliant, while the dungeon is filled with a heavenly light, as when Zeus came to Danaë in a golden shower. We read in the Protovangelion Apocrypha (ch. xiv.) that when Christ was born, on a sudden there was a great light in the cave, so that their eyes could not bear it. Nearly all of the Sun-gods are represented as having been born in a cave or a dungeon. This is the dark abode from which the wandering Sun starts in the morning. At his birth a halo of serene light encircles his cradle as the Sun appears at early dawn in the East, in all its splendor. In the words of the Veda: —

Will the powers of darkness be conquered by the god of light?

And when the Sun rose, they wondered how, just born, he was so mighty, and they said: —

Let us worship again the Child of Heaven, the Son of Strength, Arusha, the Bright Light of the Sacrifice. He rises as a mighty flame, he stretches out his wide arms, he is even like the wind. His light is powerful, and his mother, the Dawn, gives him the best share, the first worship among men.

In the Rig-Veda he is spoken of as "stretching out his arms" in the heavens "to bless the world, and to rescue it from the terror of darkness."

All of the Sun-gods forsake their homes and Virgin mothers, and wander through different countries doing marvellous things. Finally, at the end of their career, the mother, from whom they were parted long before, is by their side to cheer them in their last hours. Also the tender maidens are there, the beautiful lights which flush the Eastern sky as the sun sinks in the West. The Sun is frequently spoken of as having been born of the dusky mother, the early dawn being dark or dusky.

The Mexican Virgin goddess, Sochiquetzal — the Holding up of Roses — is represented by Lord Kingsborough as receiving a bunch of flowers from the embassador in the picture of the annunciation. This brings to mind a curious tradition of the Mahometans respecting the birth of Christ. They say that he was the last of the prophets who was sent by God to prepare the way for Mahomet, and that he was born of the Virgin by the smelling of a rose. (*Antiquities of Mexico*, vol. vi., pp. 175, 176.)

APPENDIX B.

THE LEGENDARY LIFE OF BUDDHA AND ITS RELATION TO THE INDIAN ZODIAC.

THAT the Buddhist zodiac plays a very prominent part in the legendary life of Buddha is very evident. Buddha was born on Christmas day, the new birth of the sun. The zodiacal sign for December is an elephant issuing from a Makara or Leviathan. Leviathan is one of the symbols of the first person of the triad. The elephant (Mârttanda of the Rig-Veda) is the symbol of his son, the solar God-man; therefore Buddha comes to earth in the form of an elephant. We are told that in spring, when appears the constellation Visakha (April-May), the Bodhisatwa, under the appearance of a young white elephant of six defences, with a head the color of cochineal, with tusks shining like gold, perfect in his organs and limbs, entered the right side of his mother Maha-Mâya; and she, by means of a dream, was conscious of the fact. The night on which the Bodhisatwa entered his mother's side, on that same night a huge white lotus, springing from the waters and parting the earth for sixty-eight millions of yoganas [a yogana is seven miles], rose up into the middle of the world of Brahma. This lotus, only the guide of men [Bodhisatwa] and Brahma are able to receive. All that there is of life and creative essence in the three thousand great thousand worlds [the earth] is assembled in the dewdrops of this mighty lotus.

Very early in Buddha's career the Rishi or Brahmin Asiti (the constellation Aquarius, the Waterman) pays him a visit, and immediately upon his presentation, begins to weep — weeps because he is old and stricken in years, and consequently will not live to see all the marvels the infant is to perform. Nanda and Upananda (the constellation Pisces — the two crossed fish or serpents of Buddhism, the sign Swastica), the two heavenly serpents, symbols of the father and mother of the universe, manifest themselves also at an early period. It is to be observed that Mâya, the Virgin of the sky, at the moment of Buddha's birth, midnight, December 25, was just rising above the horizon, it being the beginning of the new solar revolution. The celestial mother dies in seven days in all the Indian epics, and goes up to heaven, simply because the sun had entered Aquarius, and Virgo is rising up in the heavens. Two thousand years before Christ the sun passed the equinox under Taurus, but at the time of Buddha's birth it passed it under Aries. Hence the solar horse with the two serpents upon his head (the Buddhist Aries) is Buddha's symbol. As Makara with Aries in his mouth was the celestial sign in Palestine at the date of Christ's birth, Aries is his symbol also.

This explains the attempt made to kill the Sun-god by a wicked king (Bimbasâra in the Chinese version). When the sun is in Aries, the Buddhist shaft of death (Sagittarius) is just rising above the horizon at midnight.

Whilst in the earlier mansions of his career, the seven Rishis (Ursa Major) are near the zodiacal monarch. Hence the Rishis at the ploughing festival, the dispute with the Rishis, etc.

When the Sun-king approaches the pair (Gemini), he has to prepare for marriage. On the meridian at midnight there is now Sagittarius, and close to him Capricorn, the zodiacal elephant. Hence the invariable archery match and the attempt at the young king's life in the Indian epics, by means of an elephant. In Gemini he is united to his heavenly bride.

The palace in which the anointed Chakravartin is confined is really a prison, like that of Vishnu, as M. Stenert shows. I am convinced that the celebrated four signs are zodiacal, for the shaft of death and the Brahmachârin are plainly descernible. The old man I take to be Cancer, with his emaciated form and prominent ribs, for the simile is used when Buddha's rib-bones begin to show during his austerities. In that case, Scorpio must represent the sick man or disease.

At the commencement of summer, the Prince breaks away from his prison, the solar horse Kantaka (the name of Buddha's horse) flies out of the winter solstice. He passes into Cancer, and commences his spiritual initiation under a tree. "His body becomes terribly emaciated. His sinews and veins started out like the knotty fibres of the black sandal-tree. His ribs showed through his side like those of a CRAB."

There is no concealment of the zodiacal nature of the narrative in this passage of the *Salita Vistara*. It is to be noticed that when the sun is in the mansion of Cancer, *Swastica* (the fish) is rising above the horizon at midnight. Hence, perhaps, the convenient appearance of *Swastica*, the grass-vendor, and the kusa grass with which he supplies the Prince.

Bodhisatwa marches to the Bodihi-tree with the proud step of a LION. Here again we have the zodiacal nature of the narrative confessed. Sâkya Suñha (the lion of the Sâkyas) is gaining in spiritual vigor.

The fancy of the myth-monger is tremendously exercised by the sign Virgo. Sujata, with the rice and milk of immortality, is plainly Virgo. Mâya, the Queen of Heaven, comes also down, in an episode of the Tibetan version, to comfort her son. The tree represents the mansion Virgo in some Buddhist zodiacs. The baptism of the Prince brings in tree, water, woman, all the intricate symbolism of the subject; and that there may be no mistake, all the heavenly gods are brought in, in another episode, to administer the Abhisheka, or formal rite. The Bull is in the ascendant, when the sun is in Virgo. Hence, also, the cows with their celestial milk. After his baptism, the sun reaches the Mani, the triad symbol; so Buddha is addressed as, "O Blessed TRINITY!" The serpent Munchalinda twines round him and forms a canopy over his head. The tree overshadows him. He shines like the Sun.

Scorpio is represented by womanly tempters, by earthly appetite, the disease of the soul. And as the zodiacal king admits of no rival near his throne, he vanquishes and converts Papiyân (Sagittarius), also called Mâra or Death. Then the Chakravartin turns the Chakra of Dharma, the spiritual zodiac. The white elephant has his new birth in Capricorn, his whole birth according to the Buddhists, and commences the spiritual life. He marches along the "way" of which Buddhists make so much. His path, in fact, is the path of heaven. In the old zodiac the bloody sacrifice and dualism were accentuated. From above 2000 B.C. the sun passed the equinox under Aries, and so the solar horse in India, and the ram or lamb in the West, died for the world once a year. At the autumnal equinox, the Osiris, the Orpheus, the White Horse, entered the wintry half-year imaged by the ancients as the realms of

Pluto. Hence the great Aswamedha (horse sacrifice) of the Aryans. At the spring equinox (Easter), the sun having been wept over by virgins, rose again. But as Buddhism was a protest against the animal sacrifice, the story of the spiritual awakening of an ascetic was substituted. All this disposes, I think, of M. Stenert's theory that Buddha never lived. A new sun-myth had to be made for Buddha, and not a Buddha for a sun-myth. (*Buddha and Early Buddhism*, pp. 110-113.)

APPENDIX C.

BUDDHA AS A REFORMER.

FIVE hundred and sixty years before Christ a religious reformer appeared in Bengal — Buddha.

The following are some of the results due to the sojourn of this man upon earth: —

1. "The most formidable priestly tyranny that the world had ever seen crumbled away before his attack, and the followers were paramount in India for a thousand years.

2. "The institution of caste was assailed and overturned.

3. "Polygamy was for the first time pronounced immoral and slavery condemned.

4. "Woman, from being considered a chattel and a beast of burden, was, for the first time, considered man's equal, and allowed to develop her spiritual life.

5. "All bloodshed, whether with the knife of the priest or the sword of the conqueror, was rigidly forbidden.

6. "Also, for the first time in the religious history of mankind, the awakening of the spiritual life of the individual was substituted for religion by the body corporate. It is certain that Buddha was the first to proclaim that duty was to be sought in the eternal principles of morality and justice, and not in animal sacrifices and local formalities, invented by the fancy of priests.

7. "The principle of religious propagandism was for the first time introduced, with its two great instruments, the missionary and the preacher." (*Buddha and Early Buddhism*, pp. v., vi.)

APPENDIX D.

THE PERSIAN ACCOUNT OF THE FALL OF MAN.

ACCORDING to accounts given by Von Bolen and Dr. McCaul, the universe was created by Ormuzd in six periods of time, in the following order: First, the heavens; second, the waters; third, the earth; fourth, the trees and plants; fifth, the animals; sixth, man. After Ormuzd had finished his work he rested.

After the creation of the world the evil being (Ahriman) got upon the earth in the form of a serpent and seduced the first human pair from their allegiance to God. (See *Aids to Faith*, p. 219; also, *The Pentateuch Examined*, vol. iv. p. 113.)

Bishop Colenso tells us of the Persian legend, that the first couple lived originally in purity and innocence. Perpetual happiness was promised them by the Creator if they continued in their virtue. But an evil demon came in the form of a serpent, sent by Ahriman, the prince of devils, and gave them fruit of a wonderful tree, which imparted immortality. Evil inclinations then entered their hearts, and all their moral excellence was destroyed. Consequently they fell, and forfeited the eternal happiness for which they were destined. They killed beasts and clothed themselves in their skins. The evil demon obtained still more perfect power over their minds, and called forth envy, hatred, discord, and rebellion, which raged in the bosom of the families. (*The Pentateuch Examined*, vol. iv. p. 115.)

Ormuzd, the God of Light and of the good principle, informs Zoroaster that he had given to man a place of delight and abundance. "If I had not given him this place of delight, no other being would have done so. This place was called Eiren, which at the beginning was more beautiful than all the world, which my power had called into existence. Nothing could equal the beauty of this delightful place which I had granted. I was the first who acted, and afterwards Petiare [which is Ahriman, or the bad principle]: this Petiare Ahriman, full of death and corruption, made in the river, the great 'Adder,' the mother of winter, which congealed the water, the earth, and the trees."

It is evident that the question here is only of the physical and periodical evil which the earth experiences annually by the retreat of the Sun, which is the source of life and of light for all that live on the face of the globe. The cosmogony contains, therefore, only an allegorical picture of the phenomena of Nature, and of the influence of the celestial signs; because the serpent or the great Adder, which ushers winter into the World, is, like the Balance, one of the constellations placed on the boundaries which separate the dominion of the two principles, or, in other words, in the present instance, on the equinox of autumn.

This is the celestial Serpent or the Star Serpent. It is in the heavens that Ahriman is made to creep along under the form of a serpent. The *Boundesh*, or the Genesis of the Persians, holds the following language: "Ahriman, the principle of Evil and of Darkness, he from whom all the evil in this world is proceeding, penetrated into Heaven under the form of a serpent, accompanied by Dews, or bad Genii, whose only business is to destroy." And in another place we read: "And when the bad Genii desolated the world, and when the Star Serpent made itself a road between Heaven and Earth, or, in other words, when it rose on the horizon," etc.

Now at what epoch of the annual revolution rises the celestial Serpent, united to the Sun, on the horizon with that luminary? When the Sun has arrived at the constellation of the Balance, over which the constellation of the Serpent is extended, in other words, at the seventh sign, counting from the Lamb, or at the sign under which, as we have seen above, the Magi had fixed the commencement of the reign of the evil principle, and the introduction of Evil into the Universe.

"The cosmogony of the Jews," says Mr. Dupuis, "introduces the Serpent with a man and a woman. In it the Serpent is made to speak; but one feels that this is peculiar to the Oriental genius, and belongs to the character of the allegory. The foundation of the theology is absolutely the same. It is quite true there is no mention made by the Jews about the Serpent having introduced winter, which destroyed all the blessings of Nature; but it is said there that man felt the necessity of covering himself, and that he was compelled to till the ground, an operation which is performed in and which corresponds to autumn. It is not said that it was at the seventh thousand or under the seventh sign when the change happened in the situation of man; but the action of the good principle is there divided into six times, and it is on the seventh that its rest or the cessation of its energy is placed, as well as the fall of man in the season of fruits, and the introduction of the Evil by the Serpent, the form of which was taken by the bad principle, or the Devil, in order to tempt the first mortals. They fix the locality of the scene in the same countries which are comprised under the name of Eiren, or Iran, and towards the sources of the great rivers Euphrates, Tigris, Phison, or of the Araxes: only instead of Eiren the Hebrew copyists have put Eden, as the two letters *r* and *d* in that language have a remarkable resemblance."

This cosmogonical idea has been expressed by the Magi in another form. They suppose that from time without end or from eternity, a limited period has been created, which incessantly renews itself. They divide this period into twelve thousand small parts, which they call years in allegorical style. Six thousand of these fractions belong to the principle of Good, and the other six to that of Evil; and that there may be no mistake, they make each one of these millesimal divisions, or each one thousand, correspond to one of the signs through which the Sun makes the transit during each one of the twelve months. The first one thousand, they say, corresponds to the Lamb, the second to the Bull, the third to the Twins, etc. Under these first six signs, or under the signs of the first six months of the equinoctial year, they place the reign and the beneficent action of the principle of Light, and under the other six signs they place the action of the principle of Evil. It is at the seventh sign, corresponding to the Balance, or at the first of the signs of autumn, of the season of fruits and of winter, that they place the commencement of the reign of Darkness and of Evil. This reign lasts till the return of the Sun to the sign of the Lamb, which corresponds to the month of March and to Easter. This is the foundation of their theological system about the distribution of the opposing forces of the two principles, to the action of which man is subject, during each solar revolution; this is the tree of Good and Evil near which

Nature has placed him. Let us hear their own statements.

"Time," says the author of the *Boundesh*, "is composed of twelve thousand years: the thousands belonging to God include the Lamb, the Bull, the Twins, the Cancer, the Lion, and the Ear of Corn, or the Virgin, which makes six thousand years. If we substitute for the word 'YEAR' that of the fractions or the small periods of time, and for the name of the signs, those of the months, we shall have March, April, May, June, July, and August; in other words, the beautiful months of periodical vegetation. After these thousands of God comes the Balance. Then began the career of Ahriman in the world. After that comes the Bowman, or the Sagittarius, and Afrasiab committed the Evil," etc.

If we substitute for the names of the signs of the Balance, the Scorpion, the Sagittarius, the Capricorn, the Waterman and the Fishes, the names of the months, September, October, November, December, January, and February, we shall have the six times affected by the principle of Evil and its effects, which are the hoary frosts, the snow, the winds, and the excessive rains. It will be observed that the evil Genius begins to exercise his fatal influence in September, or in the season of fruits and of apples, by the introduction of cold weather, by the destruction of plants, etc. It is then that man becomes aware of the evils which he ignored in spring and summer in the beautiful climate of the northern hemisphere.

"According to the formal expressions used in the cosmogony, it follows that the evil introduced into the World is the winter. Who shall be its redeemer? The God of spring or the Sun in its passage under the sign of the Lamb."

It is then, when fecunded by the immortal and spiritual (*intelligent*) action of the fire Ether, and by the heat of the Sun of the equinoctial Lamb, that Earth becomes a delightful abode for man.

But when the Star of day, reaching the Balance and the Celestial Serpent, or the signs of autumn, passes into the other hemisphere, then it consigns our regions, by its retreat, to the hardships of winter, to the impetuous winds, and to all the devastations which the destructive Genius of Darkness commits in the world. There is no more hope for man, except the return of the Sun to the sign of Spring or to the Lamb, being the first of the signs. This is the Redeemer which he expects.

The Hebrew doctors themselves, as well as the Christian doctors, agree that the books which we attributed to Moses were written in the allegorical style, that they frequently represent quite a different meaning than the literal sense would indicate, and that it would lead to false and absurd notions of the Deity if we should hold on to the rind which covers sacred science. It is principally the first and second chapters of Genesis that they have acknowledged to contain a hidden and allegorical sense, of which they say we must carefully abstain from giving the interpretation to the vulgar. Maimonides, the wisest of the Rabbies, says:—

We must not understand or take in a literal sense what is written in the book on the creation, nor form of it the same ideas which are participated by the generality of mankind; otherwise our ancient sages would not have so much recommended to us to hide the real meaning of it, and not to lift the allegorical veil which covers the truth contained therein. When taken in its literal sense, that work gives the most absurd and most extravagant ideas of the Deity. Whosoever should divine its true meaning ought to take great care in not divulging it. This is a maxim repeated to us by all our sages, principally concerning the understanding of the work of the six days. It is possible that somebody, either through himself or by means of the light obtained from others, may succeed to divine its meaning; then let him be silent, or if he speaks of it, let it be done only in as veiled a manner as I do, leaving the remainder to be guessed by those who can hear me.

Maimonides adds that the enigmatical talent was not peculiar to Moses or to the Jewish doctors, but that they held it in common with all the wise men of antiquity. Philo, a Jewish writer, held the same opinion of the character of the sacred books of the Hebrews (see his treatise on the *Allegories*). "It is acknowledged by all," says Origenes, "that everything there is wrapped up under the veil of enigma and parable." Augustine, in his *City of God*, acknowledges that many people saw in the incident of Eve and the Serpent, as well as in the terrestrial Paradise, only an allegorical fiction. (See *Origin of All Religious Belief*, pp. 219, 226, 231.)

APPENDIX E.

THE LEGEND OF THE TRAVELS OF ISIS, OR THE MOON.

The ancient Egyptians associated the Moon in the universal administration of the World with the Sun, and it is the former which plays the part of Isis in the sacred fable known as the history of Osiris and Isis. We are informed by Diodorus, of Sicily, that the first inhabitants of Egypt, while admiring the spectacle of the heavens and the wonderful order of the world, thought to perceive in heaven two principal and eternal causes, or two grand divinities; and one of them they called Osiris, or the Sun, and the other Isis, or the Moon. This is confirmed by Porphyrius, Chæremon, and by other authors. The legend of Osiris and Isis has come down to us in a mutilated form, and the following is what Plutarch supposes it to have been:—

After his return from his travels in Egypt, Osiris was invited by Typhon, his brother and rival, to a banquet. He was put to death by the latter, and his body thrown into the Nile. "The Sun," says Plutarch, "occupied then the sign of the Scorpion, and the Moon was full; the latter was therefore in the sign opposite to the Scorpion; in other words, in the Bull, which lent its form to the equinoctial vernal Sun, or to Osiris, because at that remote period the Bull was the sign which corresponded to the equinox of spring." As soon as Isis was informed of the death of Osiris, she went in search of his body. She is informed by children that the coffin containing the body of her husband had been carried by the flood down to the sea, and thence to Byblos, where it stopped; that it rested quietly on a plant, which all at once had budded and put forth a splendid stem. The coffin was so completely enveloped by it, that it seemed to form only one and the same body. The king of the country, astonished at the beauty of the tree, had cut it down and made out of it a column for his palace without perceiving the coffin. Isis, informed by Fame and impelled as it were by divine instinct, arrives at Byblos. Bathed in tears, she sits down near a fountain, where she remains until the women of the queen arrive. She salutes them respectfully, and dresses their hair, so as to emit with their bodies the fragrance of an exquisite perfume. The queen, having been informed of this, and smelling the delightful fragrance of Ambrosia, desired to see the stranger. She invites Isis to come to the palace and be the nurse of her son. During the night Isis burns all the mortal parts of the child's body. At the same time she metamorphoses herself into a swallow; she flutters around the column, and fills the air with her plaintive cries, until the queen, who had observed her, shrieks with horror at the sight of her son in flames. This scream breaks the charm which would have given immortality to the infant. The goddess then made herself known, and requested that the precious column should be given up to her. She took easily from it the body of her husband, by disengaging the coffin from the wood which covered it. She veiled it with a light tissue, which she perfumed with essences; afterwards she restored to the king and to the queen this envelope of foreign wood, which was deposited in the temple of Isis at Byblos. The goddess then approached the coffin, bathing it with tears, and uttered such a terrific scream that the youngest son of the king died of terror. Isis took the oldest one with her, and embarked on board of a vessel, taking with her the precious coffin; but towards morning, a somewhat strong wind having risen on the river Phædrus, it made her stop suddenly. Isis retires aside, and supposing herself alone, she opens the coffin, and pressing her lips on those of her husband, she kisses and bedews him with her tears. The young prince, whom she had brought along with her, approached her stealthily from behind with as little noise as possible, and spied her movements. The goddess perceived it, and turning around suddenly, she gives him such a terrible look that he dies of terror. She embarks again, and returns to Egypt, near her son Orus (Horus), who was brought up at Butos, and she deposits the corpse in a retired place. Typhon, having gone hunting at night, discovers the coffin, and having recognized the corpse, he cuts it into fourteen pieces, which he throws around in all directions. The goddess having seen it, goes to collect these scattered pieces. She buries each one in the place where she had found it. However, of all the parts of the body of Osiris, the only one which she could not find was that of generation. In place of it she substitutes the phallus, which was its image, and which was consecrated to the mysteries.

Some time afterwards, Osiris returned from the infernal regions to the rescue of his son Orus, and placed him in a condition to defend him. He mounted him, some say on a horse, others on a wolf. Typhon was vanquished; Isis let him escape. Orus felt indignant on that account and took from his mother her diadem; but Mercurius gave her in its place a helmet in the shape of a bull's head.

Dupuis gives comparative pictures of the legend and the state of the heavens from the time when the sun has quitted our hemisphere, and left to the Moon, then full, the reign of the long nights, until the time when it repasses to our climes. (See *Origin of All Religious Belief*, pp. 99-107.)

APPENDIX F.

AN EXPLANATION OF THE HERACLEID, OR OF THE SACRED POEM ON THE TWELVE MONTHS AND ON THE SUN, WORSHIPPED UNDER THE NAME OF HERCULES.

The following comparison of the legend of Hercules with the constellations which preside over the twelve months is from Dupuis. (See *Origin of All Religions*, pp. 87–93.)

Whatever may have been the opinions about Hercules, he was surely not a petty Grecian prince, renowned for his romantic adventures. It is the mighty luminary, which animates and fructifies the universe, the divinity which has been honored everywhere by the erection of temples and altars, and consecrated in religious song by all nations. From Meroë in Ethiopia, and Thebes in Upper Egypt, to the British Isles and to the snows of Scythia; from ancient Taprobane and Palibothra in the Indies to Cadiz and the shores of the Atlantic Ocean; from the forests of Germany to the burning sands of Lybia, — wherever the blessings of the Sun were experienced, there the worship of Hercules is found established, there are sung the glorious deeds of this invincible God. Many centuries before the epoch which is assigned to the son of Alcmena or to the supposed hero of Tirynthia, as the time when they made him live, Egypt, Phœnicia, — which surely did not borrow their gods from Greece, — had erected temples to the Sun under the name of Hercules, and had carried his worship to the island of Thasos and to Cadiz, where they had consecrated a temple to the Year and to the Month, which divided it into twelve parts; or, in other words, to the twelve labors or twelve victories which conducted Hercules to immortality.

It is under the name of Hercules Astrochyton, or of the God clad in a mantle of Stars, that the poet Nonnus designates the Sun-god worshipped by the Tyrians. The titles of the King of Fire, or Lord of the World and of the Planets, of nourisher of mankind, of the God whose glowing orb revolves eternally around the Earth, and who while followed in his track by the Year, the daughter of Time and mother of the Twelve Months, draws along in regular succession the seasons, which renew and reproduce themselves, are so many traits of the Sun, that we should recognize them even if the poet had not given to his Hercules the name of Helios, or the Sun.

The author of the hymns which are attributed to Orpheus describes in the most precise manner the affinity, or rather the identity, of Hercules with the Sun. The Phœnicians have consequently preserved the tradition that Hercules was the Sun-god, and that his twelve labors represented the journey of this luminary through the twelve signs of the zodiac. Porphyrius, born in Phœnicia, makes the same assertion.

"The Egyptians," says Plutarch, "thought that Hercules had his seat in the Sun, and that he travelled with it around the world." The scholiast of Hesiod tells us also "that the zodiac, in which the Sun accomplishes its annual course, is the real career which Hercules travels over in the fable of the twelve labors, and that by his marriage with Hebe, the goddess of youth, we must understand the year which renews itself at the end of each revolution."

It is evident that if Hercules is the Sun, as is shown by the above-cited authorities, the fable of the twelve labors is a solar fable which can have reference only to the twelve months and to the twelve signs, of which the Sun travels over one in each month. This inference shall become a demonstration by the comparison which we shall make of each of the labors with each one of the months, or with the signs and constellations which mark the division of time in the heavens during each of the months.

Amongst the different epochs at which formerly the year began, that of the summer solstice was one of the most remarkable. It was on the return of the Sun to this point that the Greeks fixed the celebration of their Olympic feasts, the establishment of which was attributed to Hercules; this was the origin of the most ancient era of the Greeks. We shall therefore fix the departure of the Sun Hercules there, in its annual route. The sign of the Lion, domicil of that star which furnishes it with its attributes, having formerly occupied that point,— his first labor shall be his victory over the Lion; and it is indeed the one which has been placed at the head of all the others.

But before we shall compare month for month, the series of the twelve labors with that of the stars, which determine and mark the annual route of the Sun, it is well to observe that the ancients, in order to regulate their sacred and rural calendars, employed not only the signs of the zodiac, but more frequently also remarkable stars, placed outside of the zodiac, and the various constellations, which, by their rising and setting, indicate the place of the Sun in each sign. The proof of this will be found in the *Fastes* of Ovid, in Columella, and chiefly in the ancient calendars which we have published as a sequel to our larger work.

CALENDAR.	POEM.
FIRST MONTH.	TITLE OF THE FIRST CANTO OR OF THE FIRST LABOR.
Passage of the Sun under the sign of the celestial Lion, called the Lion of Nemea, fixed by the setting in the morning of the *Ingeniculus*, or the constellation of the celestial Hercules.	Victory of Hercules over the Nemean Lion.
SECOND MONTH.	**SECOND LABOR.**
The Sun enters the sign of the Virgin, marked by the total setting of the celestial Hydra, called the Lernean Hydra, the head of which rises again in the morning with the Cancer.	Hercules stays the Lernean Hydra, the heads of which grew again, whilst he is cramped in his labor by a crawfish or Cancer.
THIRD MONTH.	**THIRD LABOR.**
Passage of the Sun at the commencement of Autumn to the sign of the Balance, fixed by the rising of the celestial Centaur, the same whose hospitality Hercules enjoyed. This constellation is represented in the Heavens with a leather bottle, filled with wine, and a thyrsus adorned with vine leaves and grapes, image of the season's product. Then rises in the evening the celestial Bear, called by others the Boar and the animal of Erymanthia.	A Centaur gives hospitality to Hercules; his fight with the Centaurs for a cask of wine; victory of Hercules over them; he slays a terrible wild Boar which devastated the fields of Erymanthia.

FOURTH MONTH.

The Sun enters the sign of the Scorpion, fixed by the setting of Cassiope, a constellation which was formerly represented by a Hind.

FIFTH MONTH.

The Sun enters the sign of the Sagittarius, consecrated to the goddess Diana, whose temple was at Stymphalia, in which the Stymphalian birds were to be seen. This passage is fixed by the rising of three birds,—the Vulture, the Swan, and the Eagle,—pierced by the arrow of Hercules.

SIXTH MONTH.

Passage of the Sun to the sign of the Goat or the Capricorn, the son of Neptune, according to some, and grandson to the Sun, according to others. This passage is marked by the setting of the river of the Aquarius, which flows under the stable of the Capricorn, and the source of which is in the hands of Aristeus, son of the river Peneus.

FOURTH LABOR.

Triumph of Hercules over a Hind with golden horns and feet of brass, which Hercules took on the seashore, where it was reposing.

FIFTH LABOR.

Hercules gives chase, near Stymphalia, to the Birds of the Stymphalian Lake, which are represented in No. 3 in the medals of Perinthus.

SIXTH LABOR.

Hercules cleans the stables of Augias, the son of the Sun, or, according to others, the son of Neptune. He makes the river Peneus run through it.

SEVENTH MONTH.

The Sun enters the sign of Waterman or Aquarius, and at the place in the Heavens where the full Moon was found every year, which served to denote the epoch for the celebration of the Olympic games. This passage was marked by the Vulture, placed in the Heavens alongside the constellation called Prometheus, at the same time that the celestial Bull, called the Bull of Pariphae and of Marathon, culminated in the meridian, at the setting of the Horse Arion or Pegasus.

EIGHTH MONTH.

Passage of the Sun to the sign of the Fishes, fixed by the rising in the morning of the celestial Horse, the head of which is bearing on Aristeus, or on the Aquarius, the son of Cyrene.

NINTH MONTH.

The Sun enters the sign of the Ram, consecrated to Mars, and which is also called the Ram of the Golden Fleece. This passage is marked by the rising of the ship Argo, the set-

SEVENTH LABOR.

Hercules arrives at Elis. He was mounted on the horse Arion; he drags along with him the Bull of Creta, beloved by Pasiphae, which afterwards ravaged the plains of Marathon. He institutes the celebration of the Olympic games, where he is the first to enter the lists; he kills the Vulture of Prometheus.

EIGHTH LABOR.

Hercules makes the conquest of the Horses of Diomedes, the son of Cyrene.

NINTH LABOR.

Hercules embarks on board the ship Argo, in order to make the conquest of the Ram of the Golden Fleece. He fights with martial women, daughters of Mars, from whom he takes a

ting of Andromeda, or of the celestial Woman and of her Girdle; by that of the Whale; by the rising of Medusa, and by the setting of the Queen Cassiope.

TENTH MONTH.

The Sun leaves the ram of Phrixus and enters the sign of the Bull. This transit is marked by the setting of Orion, who was in love with the Atlantides or Pleiades; by that of Bootes, the driver of the Oxen of Icarus; by that of the river Eridanus; by the rising of the Atlantides, and by that of the Goat, the wife of Faunus.

ELEVENTH MONTH.

The Sun enters the sign of the Twins, which transit is indicated by the setting of the Dog Procyon, by the cosmical rising of the Great Dog, followed by the stretching out of the Hydra and by the rising in the evening of the celestial Swan.

TWELFTH MONTH.

The Sun enters the sign of the Cancer, which corresponds with the last month, indicated

magnificent girdle, and liberates a Maiden exposed to a Whale or a Sea-monster, like the one to which Andromeda, the daughter of Cassiope, was exposed.

TENTH LABOR.

Hercules, after his voyage with the Argonauts, in order to conquer the Ram, returns to Hesperia to make the conquest of the Oxen of Geryon; he also kills a tyrannical Prince who persecuted the Atlantides, and arrives in Italy at the house of Faunus at the rising of the Pleiades.

ELEVENTH LABOR.

Hercules conquers a terrible Dog, the tail of which was a Serpent, and the head of which was bristling with serpents; he defeats also Cygnus, or the Prince Swan, at the time in which the Dog-star scorches the Earth with its fire.

TWELFTH LABOR.

Hercules travels in Hesperia in order to gather Golden Apples guarded by a Dragon, by the setting of the Stream of the Waterman and of the Centaur; by the rising of the Shepherd and his Sheep, at the time when the constellation of the Hercules Ingeniculus is descending towards the occidental regions called Hesperia; followed by the Polar Dragon, the guardian of the Apples growing in the garden of the Hesperides; which dragon he puts under his feet, as marked in the sphere, and which falls near him towards the setting.

which, in our spheres, is near the pole; according to others, to carry off sheep with a Golden Fleece. He is preparing to make a sacrifice, and puts on a robe dyed in the blood of a Centaur whom he had slain at the passage of a river. By this robe he is consumed with fire; he dies, and ends thus his mortal career, in order to resume his youth in Heaven, and to enjoy there immortality.

REFERENCE NOTES.

NOTE 1. For accounts of Crishna, see the Vishnu Purana, pp. 491–665, trans. by Wilson; London, 1840. Maurice, History of Hindostan, vol. i., p. 283; vol. ii., pp. 324–479, 497, 563; London, 1802. Maurice, Indian Antiquities, vol. i., pp. 112, 113; vol. ii., p. 149; vol. iii., pp. 45–48, 95; London, 1874. Asiatic Researches, vol. i., pp. 259–261, 273. Higgins, Anacalypsis, vol. i., pp. 129–134; London, 1836. Joguth Chunder Gangooly, Life and Religion of the Hindoos, p. 134; Boston, 1860. Bhăgăvat-Gēētā: Cox, The Mythology of the Aryan Nations, vol. ii., pp. 105, 130, 133, 137; London, 1870. Doane, Bible Myths, pp. 498, 499; New York, 1883. Müller, The Origin and Growth of Religion, pp. 230, 261, 361; London, 1873. Prichard, An Analysis of Egyptian Mythology, pp. 283–292; London, 1873. Rawlinson, Religion of the Ancient World, pp. 126–149; London. Williams, Hinduism, pp. 108–110, 144, 215; London, 1877. Bonwick, Egyptian Belief, p. 168; London, 1878. Child, Progress of Religious Ideas, vol. i., p. 72; New York, 1855. Williams, Hinduism, pp. 110, 119. Fiske, Myths and Myth-Makers, pp. 104–107; Boston, 1877.

NOTE 2. For legends of the Hindoos, see Williams, Indian Wisdom, p. 324; London, 1875. Gross, The Heathen Religion, p. 124; Boston, 1856. Allen, India Ancient and Modern, pp. 382, 383; London, 1856. Maurice, Indian Antiquities, vol. i., pp. 125–127; vol. iv., p. 372; London, 1867. Tod, History of Rajapoutane, p. 581. Colenso, The Pentateuch Examined, vol. iv., p. 153. Chambers' Encyclopædia, art. Cherubim. Smith, Comprehensive Dictionary of the Bible, art. Cherubim. Priestley, Comparison of the Institutes of Moses with the Hindoos and Other Ancient Nations, pp. 35–49; Northumberland, 1799. Fergusson, Tree and Serpent Worship, p. 13; London, 1868. Wake, Phallicism in Ancient Religions, pp. 46, 47. Baring-Gould, Legends of the Patriarchs and Prophets, p. 148; New York, 1872. Maurice, History of Hindustan, vol. i., p. 408; vol. ii., pp. 227 *et seq*. Child, Progress of Religious Ideas, vol. i., p. 3; Mâhabhârata.

NOTE 3. For accounts of Buddha, see Rgya-Cher-rol-pan, pp. 61, 63, 69–82, 81, 97, 113, 178, 214, 259, 355, 374; Wasseljew, p. 95; Lotus, pp. xiv., xv., 82, 102, 104, 130; v., p. 106. Bunsen, The Angel Messiah, pp. 45–48; London, 1880. Müller, An Introduction to the Science of Religion, pp. 28, 244. Hardy, Eastern Monarchism, pp. 6, 62, 230; London, 1860. Hardy, The Legends and Theories of the Buddhists compared with History and Science, pp. 40, 50, 52, 134; London, 1866. Beal, Romantic History of Buddha, pp. 244–256; London, 1875. Rhys-Davids, Buddhism, pp. 36, 53, 129–204; London, 1881. Lillie, Buddha and Early Buddhism, pp. 68–179; London, 1881. Lefmann, pp. 21, 51, 124. Buddhist Birth-Stories, vol. i., pp. 69, 74, 113. Mâra, Köppen, vol. i., pp. 88, 94, 114. Seydel, pp. 163, 281. Dhammapada, vol. vii., pp. 33, 334. Huc's Travels. Burnouf, Divya-Avadâna. Oswald, Secret of the East, pp. 135, 137; Boston, 1883. Foucaux, p. 304. Sutta-Napatha, vol. iii.,

p. 11. St. Hilaire, p. 44. Higgins, Anacalypsis, vol.? p. 159. Bulfinch, Age of Fable, p. 432; Boston, 1870. Doane, Bible Myths, pp. 202, 371. Asiatic Researches, vol. iii., pp. 285, 286. King, Gnostics and their Remains, p. 167; London, 1884. Mahâvagga, p. 16. Gâtha, pp. 53, 143, 165. Plath, vol. ii., p. 2. Fuman, Ancient Faiths and Modern, pp. 82 *et seq.*; New York, 1876. Müller, A History of Ancient Sanscrit Literature; London, 1860. Fergusson, Tree and Serpent Worship, pp. 56, 113; London, 1868. Bunsen, The Angel Messiah, p. 33; London, 1880.

NOTE 4. For accounts of Mithra, see Lundy, Monumental Christianity, p. 167; New York, 1876. Dupuis, The Origin of All Religious Belief, pp. 246, 247; trans. from the French, New Orleans, 1872. Higgins, Anacalypsis, vol. i., p. 218; vol. ii., pp. 58, 59, 65, 99. Renan, Hibbert Lectures, p. 33. Bonwick, Egyptian Belief, p. 240. King, Gnostics and their Remains, pp. 47, 51. Higgins, Celtic Druids, p. 163; London, 1827. Child, Progress of Religious Ideas, vol. i., pp. 3, 272, 279. The Angel Messiah, p. 287. Colenso, The Pentateuch Examined, vol. iv., p. 153; London, 1863. Doane, Bible Myths, 376. Bunce, Fairy Tales, p. 18; New York, 1878. Dunlap, Mysteries of Adoni, p. 139; London, 1861. Baring-Gould, Legends of the Patriarchs and Prophets, pp. 17, 18; New York, 1872. Müller, A History of Ancient Sanscrit Literature, pp. 405 *et seq.* Asiatic Researches, vol. v., p. 270. Williams, Hinduism, pp. 24, 176, 214. Rawlinson, Herodotus, p. 171. Westropp, Ancient Symbol Worship, pp. 25, 47. Müller, Chips from a German Workshop, vol. ii., pp. 277, 290; London, 1876. Knight, Ancient Art and Mythology, p. 156; Boston, 1876.

NOTE 5. For accounts of Osiris, Horus, Isis, Neith, and Sarapis, see the following authorities: Prichard, An Analysis of Egyptian Mythology, pp. 55-109. Bonwick, Egyptian Belief, pp. 140-186, 261, 287, 396, 404, 412. Renouf, Religion of Ancient Egypt, pp. 83-93. Kenrick, Ancient Egypt under the Pharaohs, vol. i., pp. 283, 424; New York, 1852. Higgins, Anacalypsis, vol. i., pp. 138, 304; vol. ii., pp. 99, 102. Maurice, Indian Antiquities, vol. i., p. 127; vol. ii., pp. 14, 219. Rawlinson, Hibbert Lectures, p. 105. The History of Herodotus, book ii., pp. 170, 171; New York, 1871. Baring-Gould, Legends of the Patriarchs and Prophets, p. 19. Septhenes, The Religion of the Ancient Greeks, p. 214; trans. from the French; London, 1788. King, Gnostics and their Remains, p. 71, note, p. 109. Draper, History of the Conflict between Religion and Science, pp. 47, 48; New York, 1876. Cory, Ancient Fragments, pp. 80, 81; London, 1876. The History of Cornelius Tacitus, book v., ch. iii.; London, 1831. Knight, Ancient Art and Mythology, p. 98; New York, 1874. Goldziher, Mythology among the Hebrews, pp. 22, 127, 320, 322, 392, 446; London, 1877. Rawlinson, The Religions of the Ancient World, pp. 17 *et seq.*; London. Fergusson, Tree and Serpent Worship, p. 5. Inman, Ancient Faiths embodied in Ancient Names, vol. i., p. 159; vol. ii., pp. 284, 679, 767, 831; London, 1872. Squires, The Serpent Symbol, pp. 39, 78; New York, 1851. Oort, Bible for Learners, vol. i., p. 301; Boston, 1878. Müller, Origin and Growth of Religion, p. 130; London, 1873. Cox, The Mythology of the Aryan Nations, vol. ii., pp. 115, 125, 157; London, 1870. Dupuis, The Origin of All Religions, pp. 73, 256, 263, 397. Child, Progress of Religious Ideas, pp. 257, 259. Renouf, The Story of Ancient Egypt, pp. 34, 35; New York, 1887.

Gross, Heathen Religion, pp. 122, 123; Boston, 1856. Dunlap, Vestiges of the Spirit History of Man, pp. 35, 40, 108; New York, 1858. Dunlap, The Mysteries of Adoni, pp. 124, 125; London, 1861. Murray, Manual of Mythology, pp. 347, 348; New York, 1876. Inman, Ancient Pagan and Modern Christian Symbolism, pp. 13, 14, 50; London, 1869.

NOTE 6. For authorities quoted in account of Hercules, see Steinthal's Legend of Samson in Goldziher's Hebrew Mythology, pp. 392–419, also pp. 22, 137, 138. Volney, Researches in Ancient History, p. 41, also note on p. 42. Murray, Manual of Mythology, pp. 124, 247–263. Bulfinch, Age of Fable, pp. 200, 201. Dillaway, Roman Antiquities, p. 124; New York, 1876. Cox, Mythology of the Aryan Nations, vol. i., pp. 84, 107; vol. ii., pp. 47, 48, 72; London, 1870. Cox, Tales of Ancient Greece, p. xxvi., xxvii., 69 *et seq.*; London, 1880. Montfaucon, l'Antiquité Expliquée, vol. i., p. 213; Paris, 1772. Herodotus, book ii., chap. xiv.; New York, 1871. Chambers' Encyclopædia, art. Hercules. Cory, Ancient Fragments, p. 36, note; London, 1876; Monumental Christianity, p. 399. Oort, Bible for Learners, vol. i., pp. 414–422, 416. Knappert, The Religion of Israel, p. 61; Boston, 1878. Inman, Ancient Faiths embodied in Ancient Names, vol. ii., p. 679. Doane, Bible Myths, p. 73, note 2. Volney, Ruins, p. 41. Williams, Hinduism, pp. 108, 167. Asiatic Researches, vol. v., p. 270. Buckley, Cities of the World, pp. 41, 42. Smith, Assyrian Discoveries, pp. 167, 265; New York, 1875. Smith, Chaldean Account of Genesis, p. 174; New York, 1876. Knight, Ancient Art and Mythology, p. 92. Tacitus, Annals, book ii., ch. lix.; London, 1831. Maurice, Indian Antiquities, vol. ii., p. 155. Kreightley, The

Mythology of Ancient Greece, p. 215; New York, 1843. King, Gnostics and their Remains, pp. 48–70. Prichard, An Analysis of Egyptian Mythology, pp. 49, 50, 75, 95, 113, 119. Giles, Hebrew and Christian Records, p. 86 *et seq.*; London, 1853. Socrates, Ecclesiastical History, book v., ch. xxii., London, 1630. Higgins, Anacalypsis, vol. i., pp. 237–243. Taylor, Diegesis, pp. 214, 232. Dupuis, Origin of All Religious Belief, pp. 237–257. Lundy, Monumental Christianity, p. 399. Dunlap, Mysteries of Adoni, pp. 94–96. Cox, The Mythology of the Aryan Nations, vol. i., pp. 84, 107; vol. ii., pp. 47, 48. Child, Progress of Religious Ideas, vol. i., p. 214. Inman, Ancient Faiths and Modern, p. 304; New York, 1876. Faber, Origin of Pagan Idolatry, vol. i., p. 443; Fergusson, Tree and Serpent Worship, pp. 10, 13, 31.

NOTE 7. For accounts of Bacchus, see Dupuis, Origin of All Religious Belief, pp. 80–175, 257, 352. Higgins, Anacalypsis, vol. i., pp. 221, 305, 322, 328; vol. ii., pp. 19, 102. Prichard, An Analysis of Egyptian Mythology, pp. 3, 21, 63, 70. Taylor, Diegesis, pp. 12, 187, 191, 212, 213. Hymns of Orpheus. King, Gnostics and their Remains, p. 49. Oort, Bible for Learners, vol. iii., p. 67. Bell's Pantheon, vol. i., p. 118, art. Bacchus. Montfaucon, l'Antiquité Expliquée, vol. i., p. 211; Paris, 1722. Faber, Origin of Pagan Idolatry, vol. i., p. 443. Inman, Ancient Faiths and Modern, p. 304; London, 1876. Bulfinch, Age of Fable, p. 220; Boston, 1870. Cox, Tales of Ancient Greece, p. xxxii.; London, 1876. Higgins, Celtic Druids, p. 127; London, 1827. Bonwick, Egyptian Belief, p. 212; London, 1878. Lundy, Monumental Christianity, p. 125. Dunlap, Vestiges of the Spirit History of Man, p. 217; New York, 1858. Taylor, Eleusinian and

Bacchic Mysteries. Rawlinson, The Religions of the Ancient World.

Note 8. For accounts of the Scandinavian gods and goddesses, see Mallet, Northern Antiquities. Goldziher, Mythology among the Hebrews, p. 430. Knight, Ancient Art and Mythology, p. 85. Chambers' Encyclopædia, art. Yule. Bulfinch, Age of Fable.

Note 9. For accounts of Ostâra and the Ancient Druids, see Higgins, Anacalypsis, vol. ii., pp. 59, 99, 108, 109–259. Chambers' Encyclopædia, art. Easter. Dupuis, Origin of All Religious Belief, pp. 237, 257. Higgins, Celtic Druids, p. 163; Taylor, Diegesis, pp. 167, 184. Lundy, Monumental Christianity, p. 167. Forlong, Rivers of Life, or Faiths of Men, vol. i., p. 355; London, 1883. Bulfinch, Age of Fable.

Note 10. For authorities on China, see Semedo, History of China, p. 289. Thornton, History of China, vol. i., pp. 30, 137; London, 1844. Higgins, Anacalypsis, vol. ii., p. 227. Child, Progress Religious Ideas, vol. i., pp. 206–210. Colenso, Pentateuch Examined, vol. iv., p. 152. Baring-Gould, Legends of the Patriarchs and Prophets, p. 28. Doane, Bible Myths, p. 14. Gross, The Heathen Religion, p. 60; Boston, 1856. Cutzlaff's Voyages, p. 154. Legge, The Religions of China.

Note 11. For accounts of Quetzalcoatle, see Kingsborough, Mexican Antiquities, vol. vi., pp. 5, 166, 167, 176, 220, 361, 369; London, 1831. Amberly, Religious Belief, pp. 49 *et seq.*; New York, 1877; Squires, The Serpent Symbol, pp. 161, 175; Brinton, Myths of the New

World, pp. 95, 180, 181, 203, 204; New York, 1868. Lundy, Monumental Christianity, p. 393. Inman, Ancient Faiths and Modern, pp. 33-37; New York, 1876. Baring-Gould, Legends of the Patriarchs and Prophets, p. 119. Westropp, Ancient Symbol Worship. Humboldt, Researches, vol. i., p. 91; London, 1814. Prescott, History of the Conquest of Mexico, vol. i., p. 60; Philadelphia, 1873. Fergusson, Tree and Serpent Worship, p. 37; London, 1868. Acosta, The Natural and Moral History of the Indies, p. 513; London, 1604. Forlong, Rivers of Life, vol. i., pp. 94, 143, 242; vol. ii., pp. 94, 490, 499, 501. Réville, The Native Religions of Mexico and Peru.

NOTE 12. For accounts of Indian Saviours, see Squires, Serpent Symbol, pp. 187-192. Schoolcraft, Notes of the Iroquois. Forlong, Rivers of Life, vol. i., pp. 496, 497, 501.

NOTE 13. For accounts of Tammuz or Adonis (Adonai in Hebrew), see Prichard, Ancient Egyptian Mythology, pp. 64-66. King, Gnostics, p. 102. Cox, The Mythology of the Aryan Race, vol. ii., pp. 84, 113, 125. Inman, Ancient Faiths embodied in Ancient Names, vol. ii., pp. 213, 350. Lundy, Monumental Christianity, pp. 216, 224. Doane, Bible Myths, p. 220. Colenso, Lectures, pp. 297. Higgins, Anacalypsis, vol. ii., pp. 99, 114. Colenso, The Pentateuch Examined, vol. i., p. 115, App. Dupuis, Origin of All Religious Belief, pp. 161, 233. Taylor, Diegesis, pp. 162-164. Gross, The Heathen Religion, p. 287. Dunlap, Vestiges of the Spirit History of Man, p. 216. Dunlap, The Mysteries of Adoni, p. 23. Dunlap, Sod the Son of the Man, pp. vii., 39; London, 1861. Müller, Introduction to the Science of Religion, p. 186. Ezekiel viii., 14; Jeremiah xliv. 16-22. King, Gnostics, p. 91.

NOTE 14. For Accounts of the legends of the Chaldeans and Babylonians, see Bonwick, Egyptian Belief, pp. 28, 44. Smith, Chaldean Account of Genesis, pp. 22, 28, 29, 42, 44; New York, 1876. Smith, Assyrian Discoveries, pp. 167, 397; New York, 1875. Goldziher, Mythology among the Hebrews, pp. 316–330, 396. Murray, Manual of Mythology, p. 86. Bunsen, Angel Messiah, p. 108. Dunlap, Sod the Son of the Man, pp. 5, 6. Colenso, The Pentateuch Examined, vol. iv., p. 269. Fiske, Myths and Myth-Makers, p. 72; Boston, 1877. Müller, History of Ancient Sanscrit Literature. Williams, Indian Wisdom, p. 29; London, 1875. Rawlinson, The Religions of the Ancient World, pp. 48 *et seq*.

NOTE 15. For accounts of the Essenes, see Lillie, Buddha and Early Buddhism, pp. 58–67, 203–221. King, Gnostics, p. 23. Oswald, Secret of the East, p. 126. Ginsburg, The Essenes: Their History and Doctrines. Inman, Ancient Faiths and Modern, pp. 141, 193, 197. De Quincey, Historical and Critical Essays. Hitchcock, Christ the Spirit.

INDEX.

Abraham, 49, 63, 87.
Achilles, 73, 132, 133.
Achyuta, 151.
Aditi, 41.
Aderenedesa, 148, 150.
Adonai, 132.
Adonis, 84, 132, 133.
Afrasiab, 163.
Agathon, 111.
Agni, 127, 140.
Ahriman, 159–165.
Aithra, 151.
Alcmene, 68, 170.
Alexander, 42, 98, 125, 126.
Algonquins, 83.
Ananda, 54, 56.
Andromeda, 176.
Apis, 88.
Aquarius, 86, 154, 174, 175.
Aries, 30, 108, 132, 154, 156.
Aristeus, 174.
Aristobulus, 114, 115.
Arjuna, 39, 50.
Arusha, 151.
Aryans, 28, 29, 32, 33–36, 43, 59, 62, 88, 109, 140, 157.
Asita, 51, 154.

Asoka, 58, 91, 98, 130.
Augeas, 174.

Baal, 88.
Babel, 48, 80, 86, 87.
Bacchus, 71–73.
Bala-Rama, 49.
Baldur, 74, 139.
Ballaji, 129.
Baptism, 33, 45, 59, 61, 64, 74, 79, 85, 156.
Brahma, 44, 48, 57, 127, 153.
Buddha, 49–59, 98, 100, 109, 129, 143, 153–158.
Buddhists, 48, 49, 54, 91, 93, 97, 108, 130, 143.

Cadmus, 71.
Capricornus, 32, 49, 86, 155, 163, 174.
Cassiope, 175.
Ceres, 72.
Chandragupta, 91.
Chemosh, 88.
Christ, 30, 56, 60, 66, 68, 148, 150.
Crishna, 37–43, 49, 50, 66, 115, 128, 129, 151.

Cross, 32–34, 40, 45, 63, 74, 79, 85, 99, 109, 112, 115, 124–143.
Crucified, 31–33, 40, 73, 78, 84, 110–116, 129, 133.
Cybele, 73, 74.
Cyrene, 175.

Dahana, 41.
Danaë, 151.
Daphne, 41.
David, 74.
Deluge, 48, 61, 67, 68, 74, 77, 80, 85.
Devadatta, 52.
Devaki, 37, 41, 66, 151.
Devil, 43, 78, 81, 89, 102, 103, 143, 161.
Diana, 174.
Diomedes, 175.
Dionysius, 71.
Dove, 45, 85, 130.

Easter, 75, 76, 162.
Eden, 47, 61, 74, 76, 85, 162.
Edues, 83.
Elisha, 49.
Eopuco, 78.
Essenes, 91–100, 108, 116–119.
Eucharist, 33, 59, 61, 64, 72, 79, 85.

Faunus, 176.
Fish, 33, 45, 49, 69, 154, 155, 163, 175.

Frey, 74.
Frigga, 74.

Gautama, 57, 100.
Geryon, 176.
Gethsemane, 90.
Gnostics, 115.
Goliah, 74.
Gymnosophists, 97, 98.

Hebrews, 88, 89.
Hell or Hades, 32, 33, 40, 56, 59, 60, 65, 74, 79, 84, 89.
Hera, 68.
Hercules, 68–70, 151, 170–177.
Homer, 42.
Horus, 65, 66, 124, 148, 150, 168.

Incarnation, 34, 42, 49, 50, 82, 83, 89.
Indra, 41, 128, 129.
Io, 151.
Iokaste, 151.
Iroquois, 83.
Isaac, 49.
Isaiah, 42.
Isis, 65–67, 148, 150, 166–169.
Ixion, 73, 131, 132.
Izdubar, 87.

Jesus, 30, 60, 69, 148, 150.
Jesus Christ, 38, 66, 84, 85, 89–122, 127, 129, 132, 134, 137, 151, 152, 154.

Jonah, 49, 61.
Joshua, 49.

Kansa, 37, 38, 115, 154.
Kantaka, 53, 155.

Ladon, 71.
Lamb, 30, 33, 60, 66, 76, 108–111, 156, 161–164.

Macara, 153.
Magi, 60, 108, 147, 148, 161.
Maha-Maya, 50, 153.
Mahomet, 152.
Manco Capac, 83.
Mara, 52, 156.
Mâtanga, 50.
Mayas, 82.
Mediator, 43, 60, 83, 84.
Medusa, 176.
Meleagros, 73, 132.
Michabou, 83.
Michael, 89.
Mithras, 59, 61.
Moloch, 88.
Moses, 49, 62, 68, 71, 72, 88, 91, 93, 94, 164.
Munchalinda, 156.
Mutra, 49.
Muyscas, 82.
Mylitta, 84, 135.

Nanda, 154.
Nared, 37.
Nazarene, 98, 115.

Neith, 62, 65.
Neptune, 174.
Nigban, 57.
Nisan, 89.
Nutria, 73.

Odin, 74.
Œdipus, 151.
Ojibways, 83.
Ormuzd, 159–165.
Orpheus, 156.
Osiris, 62–65, 124, 134, 156, 166–169.
Ostara, 74.

Pantheus, 72.
Pasiphae, 175.
Pegasus, 175.
Perseus, 151.
Pharaoh, 50, 68.
Pluto, 157.
Prometheus, 73, 132, 175.

Quetzalcoatle, 77–83, 143.

Rama, 38.
Redeemer, 43, 66, 72, 163.
Resurrection, 33, 65, 72, 79, 84, 85, 89.
Rudraka, 52.

Sagittarius, 154, 163, 174.
Sais, 148, 149.
Saktideva, 49.
Sakaya Muni, 90.

Sâkya Suñha, 155.
Samson, 49, 69, 87.
Sandon, 87.
Sandracottus, 91.
Saviour, 28, 36, 41, 43, 51, 56, 66–79, 84, 100, 127, 128.
Scorpio, 156, 174.
Semele, 71.
Serapis, 68, 107, 122, 123.
Siddhârtha, 50, 91.
Siva, 44, 47, 48, 127.
Sochiquetzal, 78–81, 152.
Soma, 47.
Sujata, 156.
Swastica, 130, 140, 154, 155.
Swayambhura, 48.

Talmud, 113.
Tammuz, 84, 85, 132, 136.
Taurus, 154.
Tezcatlipoca, 77–79.
Thasos, 70, 171.
Therapeutæ, 93–98.
Theseus, 151.
Thor, 74, 138, 139, 140.

Tien, 75, 76.
Trefoil, 45, 63.
Triangle, 45, 134.
Trinity, 29, 41, 44, 64, 74, 76, 78, 83, 85, 134, 156.
Tripod, 45.
Typhon, 168.

Upananda, 154.
Uriel, 89.

Virgin, 29, 30, 36, 41, 65–84, 128, 147–156, 166–169, 173.
Vishnu, 36, 37, 41, 42, 44, 49, 129, 155.

Wittoba, 129.

Yar, 89.
Yule, 74.

Zerban, 87.
Zeus, 68, 136, 151.
Zomo, 83.
Zoroaster, 62, 160.

www.ingramcontent.com/pod-product-compliance
Lightning Source LLC
LaVergne TN
LVHW061213060426
835507LV00016B/1919